JUNGLE RODEO

Joe started across the corral, slowly. From the stable, he heard the whinny of a horse—in a cubicle near the gate, the chief sat astride a palomino. The door of the cubicle shot up, and the horse raced right for Joe as the chief gave a wild, ear-shattering whoop.

At the first sound, Joe started moving. His feet were pumping beneath him, his heart was pounding in his chest, and his lungs felt as if they would burst. He rounded the corral, approaching the gate from the opposite side, steadily getting closer.

Then he felt the rope drop down over his shoulders and tighten.

And he heard the chief's cry of triumph. "You lost, boy. You're dead!"

Books in The Hardy Boys Casefiles™ Series

No. 11 BROTHER AGAINST BROTHER
No. 12 PERFECT GETAWAY

THE HARDY BOYS

CASEFILES

NO. 12

PERFECT GETAWAY

FRANKLIN W. DIXON

AN ARCHWAY PAPERBACK
Published by SIMON & SCHUSTER

New York   London   Toronto   Sydney   Tokyo   Singapore

An Archway paperback
first published in Great Britain
by Simon & Schuster Ltd in 1992
A Paramount Communications Company

Copyright © 1988 by Simon & Schuster Inc.

Simon & Schuster Ltd
West Garden Place
Kendal Street
London W2 2AQ

THE HARDY BOYS, AN ARCHWAY PAPERBACK
and colophon are registered trademarks of Simon & Schuster Inc.

THE HARDY BOYS CASEFILES is a trademark
of Simon & Schuster Inc.

Simon & Schuster of Australia Pty Ltd
Sydney

A CIP catalogue record for this book is
available from the British Library

ISBN 0-671-71602-6

Printed and bound in Great Britain by
HarperCollins Manufacturing, Glasgow

Chapter

1

"DECK THE HALLS with boughs of holly," Frank Hardy chanted ironically, looking around at the palm trees fringing the deserted white beach on which he and his brother, Joe, stood.

"Fa-la-la-la-la-la Flor-i-da!" Joe joined in as he pushed sweat-dampened blond hair off his forehead. The sun was hot on his face. The jeans and sweatshirt he had put on in Bayport that morning were threatening to cook him. But then, when the two boys had left the North for Miami, they had taken off in a blizzard.

Frank was dressed like his younger brother, except that his sweatshirt bore two Chinese characters—his karate dojo's logo—instead of an orange varsity football letter. Frank's martial arts specialty wasn't a school sport at Bayport High, but he was very proud of his brown belt.

1

"This sure won't be a white Christmas for us unless we get this case wrapped up fast," said Frank. He, too, was sweating after the five miles they had walked on this beach to leave swimmers and sunbathers far behind.

"I'm asking Santa for a swimsuit—delivered early," said Joe. He looked up at the clear southern sky and stretched his arms wide, trying to unkink muscles still stiff from the air trip. "Are you sure we don't have time for a swim?"

"Forget it," said Frank. "This isn't a vacation."

"Don't remind me. We never take vacations. That trip to Colorado was the closest we've come in at least a year, and *that* was certainly no joyride," Joe said. The Hardys' last case had led them deep into the Colorado Rockies in pursuit of a hit man.

"You know, we *could* actually make this a vacation if we wanted," Joe continued, his blue eyes twinkling. "We could definitely afford a beach house if you'd just shake loose a little of that cash—"

"Get serious, Joe," said Frank.

"That's the problem with you, Frank," Joe said. "You're always serious. If you'd go with the flow—"

"We'd both have gone down the drain long ago," Frank said, cutting him off. "One of us has to take care of business, and it sure isn't you."

"Yeah," said Joe. "I saw the way you were

holding that bag on the flight down here." He looked down at the expensive leather attaché case that was lying on the sand next to their duffel bags. "Were you afraid I'd grab it and go on a shopping spree when we hit the Gold Coast?"

"No sense tempting you." Frank grinned. "One of the local girls might want a night on the town."

"You're right." Joe grinned back at his older brother. "But just let me take one more look inside. That's the stuff that dreams are made of."

Frank hesitated, then shrugged. "Okay," he said. "But just for a second." He squatted next to Joe in front of the case, clicked open both locks, and lifted the lid.

For a few seconds both Hardys stared at the bundles of bills neatly stacked in the case.

"Enough," said Frank, abruptly snapping it shut.

Joe was about to protest when he heard a car horn blare from behind the palm trees: once, twice, three times.

Frank looked at his watch. "Right on time," he said, his brown eyes suddenly wary.

He took a whistle from his pocket and gave three shrill blasts. The two Hardys waited. Silent. Still. A minute later a small man in a tan chauffeur's uniform appeared among the palms. With one hand he motioned for Frank and Joe to approach. In his other hand was something that turned his gesture into an absolute command: a large nickel-plated automatic, glinting in the bright afternoon sun, pointed straight at them.

When the Hardys reached him, the man with the gun spoke in a clipped British accent. "Joe and Frank, I presume."

"That's right," Frank said.

"I apologize for the informality of addressing you gentlemen by your first names, but it's company policy," the man said.

"And what's your name?" Frank asked.

The man smiled, his lips a straight, tight line. "You may call me Jeeves." He motioned them closer with his gun. "Now, if I may see your tickets, we can move on."

"Our tickets?" asked Frank.

The gun gestured toward the attaché case.

"Oh, I get it," said Frank and snapped it open.

Jeeves glanced at the contents, then nodded. "Very good, sir," he said. "We may proceed with our journey."

"Just out of curiosity," said Joe, trying not to watch the gun pointing at him, "what would have happened if we didn't have our, er, tickets? The, uh, train would have left without us?"

"Not at all, sir," Jeeves replied. "But your final destination would not have been the one you originally intended."

"I get it," Joe said, managing a grin. "A one-way trip, huh?"

"An elegant way of putting it, if I may say so, sir," said Jeeves. "And now, if there are no more questions—" He motioned for them to walk ahead of him through the palm trees.

Beyond the palms ran a blacktop road. Parked beside it was an enormous gray stretch limo. Its chrome was beautifully polished, and its dark windows gleamed.

"Climb in, gentlemen, and we'll be on our way," Jeeves said as he held open the rear door with one hand. The other hand still held the silver automatic—not pointing at them but not away from them, either.

Frank and Joe looked into the spacious interior. They could see soft leather seats, a television set, and even a built-in bar.

"You do give your customers their money's worth," said Joe. "Battleships like this are for big wheels only."

"If you'll climb in," Jeeves repeated with a hint of impatience.

"Sure, sure," said Joe, and he tossed his duffel bag into the dark interior of the car. As soon as both boys were inside, the door behind them slammed, and they heard the click of its lock.

A second later a light came on, and they could see that the two side windows, the rear window, and the plastic shield that separated the driver from them were opaque.

"I thought windows like this were supposed to keep people from looking *in* while you could still look out," said Joe. "You know, part of the lifestyle of the rich and famous."

"These windows must have been custom-made for the rich and infamous," said Frank, pressing his nose against the glass as he tried to look out the side window. He could see nothing. "Somebody doesn't want us to see where we're going."

"Actually, the rich and famous aren't the only ones who use limos like this," Joe said.

"Who else does?" asked Frank.

"Funeral directors."

Frank grimaced, then finished Joe's thought. "Let's just hope this limo isn't being used for *our* funeral."

Chapter

2

THE DAY BEFORE, a ride to their own funeral had not been one of the Hardys' worries. Their main concern was that Christmas was just a week away, and they still hadn't bought any gifts.

In the morning, after breakfast, they were in Frank's room, planning their shopping.

"Agreed, then," said Joe. "What you get for Callie is your business." He was talking about Callie Shaw, Frank's steady girlfriend.

"Right," said Frank. "And what you get for half the girls in Bayport is *your* problem."

"It's the price of success," said Joe with a mock sigh.

"And of course we won't talk about what we're getting for each other," said Frank.

"Because it won't be worth mentioning," said Joe with a grin. "Personally, I've budgeted two dollars and ninety-eight cents, tax included, for your present."

"You shouldn't have told me—it makes me feel like a tightwad. Anyway, that leaves Dad and Mom and Aunt Gertrude. We'll buy gifts for them together."

"Maybe that computer of yours can come up with some gift ideas," suggested Joe. "We need some help. In fact, *I* need some help. Can you supply a little financial first aid? Maybe make me a small loan?"

"No way," said Frank. "The last upgrade I did on the computer put me near bankruptcy."

"Yeah, like that new engine in the van did to me," said Joe.

They sat in silence for a moment. Then Frank said, "Maybe you're right. Let's see if my computer can come up with some brilliant solution."

But before he could begin, the telephone in his room rang.

"Must be Callie," he said, going to answer it.

The person on the phone was a girl, but not Callie.

"Hi, Frank, it's Marcie Miller," she said. "Hope you don't mind my calling, but I needed to talk to you. Callie didn't want to give out your number at first, but I told her it was an emergency." She hesitated. "I told her it was a life-or-death situation."

Frank was instantly alert. Callie wouldn't have

urged someone to call for no reason. She was the most levelheaded person he knew.

"What's up?" he said.

"I'd rather tell you in person, at my house," Marcie said. "Please, could you come over right away? You and Joe. I need you both. I have to have some help, or—" She broke off. The desperation in her voice made it clear how urgently she needed them.

"We'll be right over," Frank promised.

"Thanks. Please hurry," she said and hung up.

"Come on. We have to get to Marcie Miller's place. Fast," Frank said. He headed for the closet to get his coat.

Joe didn't waste time asking questions. He could see from the gleam in Frank's eye that something interesting was cooking, and his appetite for action was as keen as his brother's. He raced to his room for his coat, beat Frank downstairs, and was already behind the wheel of the van warming up the motor in the icy morning air when Frank slid into the seat beside him.

On the drive to Marcie's, there was time to talk.

"Wonder what the problem is with Golden Girl?" said Joe, using his favorite nickname for Marcie.

"I always think of her as the rich little rich girl," said Frank. "But I guess that isn't fair. It isn't Marcie's fault that she has everything."

"Yeah," said Joe. "Looks, brains, personality,

plus all the things that her platinum card can buy."

"Everything except a mother," said Frank, looking thoughtful. Marcie's mother had passed away when Marcie was born. "Maybe that's why everybody likes her. She definitely hasn't had *all* the breaks."

"She's lucky to have the kind of dad she has," said Joe, keeping his eyes on the road. Although the road had been plowed, there were still treacherous icy patches. Joe liked to drive fast, but he also drove well.

"Yeah, Mr. Miller is a real good guy—especially for a big-shot executive," said Frank. "He spends a lot of time with Marcie, talks with her, listens to her. He really tries to take the place of her mom."

"Marcie always says that she thinks he's tops," Joe agreed.

Joe parked the van beside the curb in front of Marcie's home, an imposing colonial mansion set back on a huge lawn blanketed with snow.

"We haven't been here since Marcie's Halloween party. Do you think the maid will remember us?" asked Frank.

Joe grinned as he rang the doorbell. "After the way you scared her with that fake skeleton, I don't think she'd *want* to remember you."

A young woman opened the door. It was Marcie—but this wasn't the Marcie that Frank and Joe knew. This girl was pale and unsmiling, and her movements were quick and nervous. She ushered the boys inside, then closed the door and leaned back against it. Her body sagged with relief. "Boy, am I glad to see you," she exclaimed.

"What's going on?" asked Frank.

"Come into the library and I'll show you," she said. Marcie led them down the hallway, continuing to talk as they followed her. "I never realized how big this house is until today. I can practically hear my footsteps echoing. Maybe it's because I'm almost never in it all alone. Dad's not here, today, though, and I sent the maid home."

On an antique oak table in the library was an expensive leather attaché case. Marcie snapped it open, and the Hardys' mouths dropped open.

Frank leaned closer. "Hundred-dollar bills. Are they all hundreds?"

"All of them," said Marcie. "I checked."

"That's a lot of cash," Joe finally managed to say. "What'd you do, rob a bank?"

Marcie caught her breath on a choking sob.

"Hey, sorry if I said anything wrong," Joe said hurriedly.

Marcie tried to pull herself together. "It's not your fault. You couldn't know. Nobody knows—not yet, anyway."

"Knows what?"

"About my dad," she said and buried her face in her hands, sobbing.

Frank and Joe waited. As active as they were, they knew that sometimes all they could do was wait.

Marcie calmed down after only a moment. She lifted her head from her hands, her eyes red and damp, but her face resolute. "I'm sorry. I know I can't help my dad if I go to pieces." She bit her lip, then continued in a steadier voice. "I'll tell you what happened. Then maybe you can help me make some sense out of it. And figure out what to do."

She sat down in one of the high-backed oak chairs by the table, and the Hardys sat down, too. In front of them the attaché case lay open like a question demanding an answer.

But Marcie didn't start with the money. She started with her dad.

"Let me say it fast, so I can get it out," she said. "My dad's in jail. Two plainclothes police officers came here and arrested him yesterday." She took a deep breath. "They've accused him of stealing—'embezzling' is the word they used—a fortune, millions and millions of dollars, from Maxtel. That's the company he's vice-president of. And—"

"Your dad?" said Frank, thinking of the distinguished-looking yet down-to-earth man who was Marcie's father.

"No way," said Joe, remembering when Marcie's dad had given not only money but also a lot of his own time and effort to help Marcie's high school class establish a shelter for the homeless.

"I know it, and you know it, but the law doesn't," said Marcie. "And this attaché case full of money makes it even worse."

"How so?" asked Frank, hoping the answer wasn't what he thought it might be.

"Dad called from jail early this morning and asked me to bring him some clothes and stuff, since they were holding him without bail," said Marcie. "Seems like a whole lot of big-time white-collar crooks—the same kind they say he is—have been doing vanishing acts lately, and they're not taking any chances."

"Yeah, I read about one the other day," said Joe. "Karl Ross, the takeover king. He took off."

"But what does that have to do with this money?" asked Frank.

"When I went to my dad's closet to get the clothes, I found this attaché case," said Marcie. "Normally I wouldn't have opened it, but I thought it might have something in it that he needed and forgot to tell me about. So I did. And it was a good thing. Because twenty minutes later, some cops showed up with a search warrant—and if I hadn't hidden the case in my room, they would have found it. You can imagine what it would have looked like to them."

"Yeah, I can imagine," said Frank, staring at the money.

"But you don't think—I mean, you *can't* think—" Marcie could go no further.

"Look, Marcie, he's your dad and all," Frank said gently. "But you have to see how it looks to somebody who isn't as involved."

"Don't worry, Marcie," Joe said, cutting in. "Frank always starts with the worst case. We both know your father well enough to know he's not a crook."

"Thanks, Joe," Marcie said, putting her hand on his arm. Then she turned to Frank. "Frank, I know you're not being unfair. It *does* look bad. Dad has a lawyer who can help him in court, but he needs somebody working on the outside to prove his innocence. That's why I called you two. Can you help? Will you?"

"We're not miracle workers, Marcie," Frank told her. "We'll try to find out what's going on, but we can't promise what the results will be. And if it turns out that you don't like what we find, we'll still have to tell the authorities."

"I'll take that chance," said Marcie with a glimmer of hope in her eyes for the first time. Suddenly she frowned. "The trouble is, there's practically nothing to go on. Dad says the only person who can clear him of the charges against him is the company president, Adolf Tanner. He and Tanner were trying to buy some company in South America. First the money vanished, and then Tanner vanished. What's even worse, the police think my dad had something to do with

14

both things. They hinted to Dad that he could have wanted Tanner out of the way before Tanner discovered the money was gone." She paused. "The charges against him are a lot worse than theft."

"Then our first job is to find Tanner," said Frank.

Marcie shook her head. "That's what everybody, including Dad, has been trying to do for the past week. No luck. It's as if Tanner disappeared into thin air."

For a moment silence hung over the room. Abruptly the telephone rang, and Marcie sprang to answer it.

"Hello," she said, then listened for a second. "Hold on, please." She covered the mouthpiece with the palm of her hand as she turned to the Hardys.

"It's for my dad. What should I do?"

Frank reacted instantly. "Give me the phone."

He spoke into the receiver, making his voice sound deeper and slower. "Hello, Gregory Miller here."

The woman's voice on the other end was the polite voice of a sales representative, the kind that sounded as if it had been programmed by a machine. "Hello, Mr. Miller. This is Perfect Getaway Travel, Limited. I am returning your call about our special Perfect Getaway Travel plan." She paused. "I am correct, am I not, Mr. Miller? You do want a Perfect Getaway, don't you?"

15

Chapter

3

"THAT'S RIGHT, I want to know about a Perfect Getaway," said Frank, keeping the rising excitement out of his voice. He motioned for Joe and Marcie to keep quiet as he switched on the speakerphone to let them listen in.

"Well, we here at Perfect Getaway realize that our clients are usually *very* pressed for time. I'm happy to say that we've arranged your reservation, and I'm calling to give you your itinerary," the voice said. "First of all, though, we must go over the matter of payment once again, to make sure it's completely understood."

"If we must, we must," said Frank.

"As I mentioned in our last conversation, the fee for our club will be seventy-five thousand dollars, to be paid in bills no larger than one-hundred," the woman continued smoothly.

16

"Needless to say, we cannot accept checks or credit cards."

"Of course," Frank agreed. "Now, if you'll tell me what I'm supposed to do, where I'm supposed to go."

"We will be sending you by messenger a map of southern Florida," said the woman. "On the map you will find a spot marked on a beach. That is where our representative will rendezvous with you tomorrow afternoon, if that is convenient for you."

"It's fine," said Frank. "The sooner the better."

"Most of our clients feel that way," the woman said. "Now, just one more detail. What will your name be?"

"Name?" said Frank.

"An essential part of our special Perfect Getaway plan is to leave your old self behind, including your name," said the woman. "From the moment you join us, we don't even want to *know* your old name or anything about you. In fact, we prefer to have merely a new *first* name for you. We and our clients have found that this is the best possible arrangement for all of us. In fact, after this call is completed, all record of your present name will be deleted from our files."

"I get it," said Frank. "What nobody knows can't hurt anybody."

"Exactly," the woman said. "Now, if you'll give us a name we can use for you . . ."

17

"What about—Frank? I think that has a nice ring to it."

"Fine, Frank," said the woman. "Well, if there's nothing else—"

"Uh, there's one other thing," said Frank.

"What's that?" asked the woman.

"I've got a partner," said Frank. "He's looking for a Perfect Getaway, too. In fact, he needs one very badly. May I bring him with me?"

"Please hold, sir, while I check with my supervisor," said the woman. A few moments later, she came back on the line. "Yes, we can accommodate your partner. That will be a total of one hundred fifty thousand dollars. And remember, nothing larger than hundred-dollar bills."

"No discount?" asked Frank indignantly. "A group rate, perhaps?"

"Wait a moment, I'll have to check," said the woman. Another pause followed. "Yes, we are able to offer you a special rate of one hundred twenty-five thousand dollars for two."

"That's more like it," said Frank.

"And what is your companion's name?"

"His name now or his new one?" asked Frank.

"His new one, of course," said the woman.

"Of course," said Frank. "What about, er, Joe? That should be easy for him to remember."

"Joe it is," said the voice. "Now, do you have any more questions?"

"Just one," said Frank. "What kind of clothes do we wear?"

"Dress as casually and inconspicuously as possible, for obvious reasons. And don't bother bringing much luggage. Perfect Getaway will provide you with a new wardrobe suitable for wherever your Perfect Getaway will take you."

"All included in your fee?" asked Frank, doing his best to sound like a suspicious customer.

"Of course, sir. One payment covers all."

"That sounds fine," Frank said.

"We'll do our best to take care of your every need," said the woman. "A satisfied customer is our best advertisement. As you said yourself when you contacted us, you got our name through a personal recommendation."

"Yes, that's right, I did," said Frank. "Well, so long. And thank you."

"Thank *you*," said the voice. "And we hope you have a Perfect Getaway."

There was a click, then a dial tone. Frank stared thoughtfully at the speaker in the middle of the desk before he hung up the receiver.

"So we're heading down to Florida," Joe said finally. "Great. We'll go home, pack our duffel bags, and get to the bottom of this Perfect Getaway stuff."

"Not so fast," said Frank. "I set up that meeting in Florida to keep our options open—but maybe we should tell the police about this."

Frank turned to Marcie, then hesitated. "Look, Marcie, I hate to say it, but this doesn't look good for your dad. I mean, apparently he got in touch with this Perfect Getaway outfit right before he was arrested. Plus, he had that attaché case filled with the hundreds. We may be breaking the law if we don't inform the authorities. It could be important evidence in their case against him."

Much to his relief, Marcie didn't get mad. But she also didn't give up her position.

"Dad would never try to run away from anything," she said with absolute certainty. "There has to be another explanation. And I'm not saying that just because I'm his daughter."

"Frank, let's keep our options open, as you suggested," Joe said. "There has to be something we don't know. And I say we go down to Florida and find it before we present the cops with more evidence that makes Mr. Miller look guilty."

Frank still looked doubtful. "I appreciate the way both of you feel. But feelings aren't facts."

"Right," said Joe. "That's why we should go down to Florida—to get the facts."

"You have to," pleaded Marcie. "You two are the only ones who can help clear my dad."

Frank shrugged. "Okay. We'll go for two reasons. First, I can't picture your dad as a crook. And second, I wonder if Mr. Tanner called Perfect Getaway, too."

Joe grinned at Marcie. "I had a feeling he'd go. He doesn't like sitting around doing nothing any more than I do. And if it means taking a few chances—well, it's not the first time we've done it."

Frank couldn't dispute that. But he said soberly, "I want one thing understood. If we do find out that your dad was planning on vanishing, or if we find out anything else against him, we'll have to go to the cops with what we dig up. We can't be part of a cover-up."

Marcie nodded and said, "I understand, but I know there isn't a chance in the world you'll find out anything bad about him."

"Great, we're all set," said Joe. "We've got enough cash to convince Perfect Getaway that we're genuine and even to buy our airline tickets."

"I'll take care of the tickets," said Marcie. "I'll pay for them with a credit card. I'd go down with you, except that Dad might need me around, and I'm sure you two know what you're doing."

Frank was already leafing through a telephone book looking for the phone numbers of airlines with Florida routes. "Let's hope we can get a flight. Bookings over Christmas are tight."

"You can travel first class," Marcie said. "There are always seats available there."

"Money," said Joe, picking up the attaché case. "Wonderful what it can do."

The next day, though, as Joe sat with Frank in the locked backseat of the limo speeding toward an unknown destination, he wasn't so sure about the power of money.

He patted the attaché case on the seat between Frank and him and said, "This money got us into this dungeon on wheels. Let's hope it can get us out."

Frank signaled Joe to be quiet while he turned on the car's television set. Turning up the volume, he leaned over and whispered to his brother, "Be careful. The driver may be listening to make sure that we're the right guys."

Joe nodded his understanding.

Frank continued, "Things are happening faster than I expected. I thought we'd just make contact with Perfect Getaway, then wait while they made plans. Whatever we did, I thought we'd have time to call Marcie and fill her in. That way if something went wrong, we could count on some help showing up."

"Too late for that now," muttered Joe. "One item this limo lacks is a phone in the backseat." He shivered, and it wasn't because of the air-conditioning. "We've worked without a backup before, but when we climbed into this car, I felt as if we were entering another world. Like we were cutting all ties to the past, to everything we know. Creepy, huh?"

"You're not the only one who's spooked." Frank nodded in agreement.

"I wish we'd had time to let Dad know what

we were doing," said Joe, referring to their father, the famous private detective Fenton Hardy.

"I know what you mean," answered Frank. "But it's too late now—too late to tell anyone where we are."

Joe glanced at his watch. "We've been traveling for more than an hour. Wonder how much longer it'll be?"

"Not much—unless this limo can go underwater," said Frank. "We started out going south, and the car hasn't made any turns. That should put us at the tip of Florida—or beyond."

"What do you mean, 'beyond'?" asked Joe, glad to see that Frank's powers of observation and deduction hadn't been left behind.

"This highway continues as a causeway, linking all the tiny islands that form the Florida Keys, all the way to Key West," said Frank, looking at the map of the area that Perfect Getaway had sent.

Suddenly Joe stiffened. "The car's turning," he said.

"And slowing down," added Frank as he turned off the television. "We must have left the main highway."

The car continued at a slower speed. Then, after about ten minutes, it came to a stop. They heard the driver's door open.

The Hardys waited in tense silence for the car's back door to open or for the locks to click open.

23

"Why isn't Jeeves letting us out?" Joe asked nervously.

"Maybe he's gone to check with his boss. Or to get some help. Or both," Frank said speculatively.

Another three minutes of silence passed, while Joe watched the numbers on his digital watch change.

Then the lock clicked and the car door swung open.

Jeeves was there, and with him was a tall man with his hair shorn in a military crew cut. His clothes were military, too: sharply pressed green fatigues and polished army boots, and he carried a standard M-16 infantry rifle. But when Frank looked closer, he saw no insignia of rank or unit on the man's sleeves, and no name was stenciled on the strip of white material above the shirt pocket. Whatever army he belonged to was a private one.

Frank glanced sideways at Joe. Joe was checking the guy out, too, and doubtless had reached the same conclusion.

"If you will leave the car now, gentlemen, and accompany Bob here," Jeeves said, stepping aside to let them out.

Frank and Joe climbed out of the car and found themselves standing in front of a white-columned mansion that looked like it came straight off a movie set of the old South. But there was one thing different in this set. Through the breaks in the tropical mangrove trees edging the property, the Hardys could see a high wall topped by barbed wire.

Bob saw them trying to get their bearings, and motioned with his rifle. "Let's go. No sense in you looking around here. You ain't staying. This is just your jump-off spot."

Jeeves, gun in hand once more, couldn't resist adding, "Bob is quite right. You won't be staying—unless, of course, you are here under false pretenses." He smiled, clearly pleased with himself. "In that case, this place will be your final destination." His grin grew more ghoulish. "Or should I say, your *eternal* resting place."

Chapter

4

"FIRST WE TAKE care of business," Bob told the Hardys as he pressed the buzzer to the door of the mansion. Another man in fatigues and carrying an M-16 opened the door and waved them through.

The interior was a surprise. The outside of the mansion looked straight out of the South before the Civil War, but inside everything was strictly contemporary. The lighting was indirect, the walls were painted in soft pastels, the carpeting was thick and springy underfoot, the furniture was modern and sleek. It was like walking into an expensive international-style hotel.

Bob herded the Hardys into a room that had been turned into an office, where a pretty young woman was sitting behind a free-form desk. Its top was uncluttered except for a computer.

The young woman looked up at them, smiling automatically. When she saw two teenage boys approaching her instead of the middle-aged men she had expected, the smile wavered for an instant. She quickly replaced it. "Hi. I'm Sally," she said coolly. "If you'll tell me your names, we'll get you checked in."

Frank recognized her voice. She was the one he had talked to on the phone at Marcie's.

"Hi," he said. "I think I spoke to you before. I'm Frank. And this is Joe."

"Hi, Frank and Joe," Sally said suspiciously. She punched their names into the computer and looked at the monitor screen, which Frank and Joe couldn't see. Then she said, "Glad you arrived on time. Everything is so much simpler when our clients obey instructions. That will be one hundred twenty-five thousand dollars, please."

Frank put the attaché case on the table and opened it. "Shall I count it out, or do you want to?"

"I'd be happy to, sir," Sally said.

As she picked up the first bundle of bills, her whole manner changed abruptly. The unconvincing smile vanished from her face, her eyes focused like high-intensity lights on the bills, and her fingers moved as quickly as if they were machine parts, flipping through the bills amazingly quickly. After she had counted the bundle, she separated several bills from the rest and examined them with a penlight and a magnifying glass, which she took from a drawer.

"What's the matter, don't you trust us?" Frank asked quickly, suddenly wondering himself about all those hundreds. Were they funny money?

"Nothing personal, sir, just routine," said Sally automatically, not bothering to look up. She took another bundle of bills from the case and repeated the counting and checking.

Frank and Joe waited. The only sounds in the office were the rustling of the bills and Bob clearing his throat behind them. Neither Frank nor Joe turned around, but both could picture the M-16 in his hands. And they could be sure he was holding it ready.

Finally Sally looked up from the bundles of bills piled neatly on the desk in front of her. Her smile was switched back on. Whatever doubts she might have had about Frank and Joe seemed to have vanished.

"Everything seems to be in order," she said. "Now, what do you want to do with your remaining cash?" She pointed to the bundles of bills still in the attaché case. The case was still about three-quarters full. "Would you like to deposit the money in an account with us? Or do you prefer to keep it with you?"

"If it's all the same, we'll keep it with us," said Frank.

"I understand perfectly," Sally said. "In fact,

most of our clients prefer to keep their cash on hand. We cater to a very self-reliant kind of person. Survivors, that's how we like to think of them.''

"Yes, well, it's a hard, cruel world out there. That's why we want to get away from it all," said Frank, fishing for information. "Just like all your other customers, right?"

But Sally only smiled politely and said, "Bob will show you to your suite now. I'm sure you'll want to freshen up. I hope you don't mind, but you two will have to share a suite, since you're being given a discount. Of course, if you wish to pay a bit more—"

"One suite will be fine," said Frank.

"Well, then, I hope you enjoy your stay." Sally snapped shut the attaché case and pushed it toward Frank.

Frank tried one last probe as he picked it up. "I hope this stay won't be too long. I mean, we've got to be moving."

"All in good time," she said. "There are a few formalities. But don't worry, I assure you that you won't be disturbed here. We are *very* secluded."

"Yes," said Joe. "I saw the fence out front. Can't say I liked it, though. Reminded me too much of a prison."

"It's for your own protection, sir." Sally smiled. "Bob, if you will escort our guests to their suite."

"Let's move it," said Bob. None of Sally's good manners had rubbed off on him. "You've got half an hour before your interview."

"Interview?" said Frank.

"What kind of interview?" asked Joe.

Bob cut off further conversation with a gesture of his gun.

He led them up a curving stairway and along a hall to a door on the second floor. "Make yourselves comfortable," he said. "I'll be back for you in half an hour."

Frank and Joe entered their room, and the door closed behind them. They weren't surprised to hear it being locked from the outside. They had already gotten the idea that they weren't totally trusted.

As soon as they were inside, Frank caught Joe's gaze, put his finger to his lips, then tapped that finger against his ear.

Joe got the message: just like the limo, the room might be bugged.

"You know, this place is gorgeous," Joe said in a loud voice as he began to check out one side of the room for listening devices, looking behind paintings, on the backs and bottoms of pieces of furniture, in vases, and under rugs.

"Perfect Getaway is really giving us our money's worth," said Frank, checking out the other side.

Working their way around the room, they met

on the far side, where they both shrugged and gestured to signify that they had found nothing.

Frank's eyes darted around the room, checking to see if they had missed anything. Then he glanced up and pointed at the old-fashioned chandelier hanging from the high ceiling. Joe nodded.

"I think I'll get some exercise," Frank said. "I need to work out some kinks from the trip."

"Good idea," said Joe. "Me, too."

He watched Frank get a chair and position it under the chandelier. Frank stood on the chair, then squatted down and made a stirrup with his hands. Joe nodded, recognizing a gymnastic stunt they had worked up the year before in a skit for a school show. Joe backed up a couple of steps, propelled himself forward, and leapt when he was about a yard from Frank, his right foot landing in Frank's linked hands. Frank heaved upward as Joe pushed off from his hands, and a second later Joe was standing on Frank's shoulders. Careful not to lose his balance on the chair or disturb Joe's balance on his shoulders, Frank straightened up slowly. It worked. Joe was up high enough to inspect the chandelier. He peered into it and saw a miniature black receiving device.

Joe leapt down, hit the carpet, and did a neat somersault, just to finish the routine off right. "Good workout," he said loudly. He pointed to the chandelier, put his finger to his lips, and nodded.

"Time for a nice, hot shower," said Frank. He went into the bathroom, and Joe followed him.

"Great shower, needle-point spray!" Frank shouted, as if Joe were still in the other room.

He then closed the door and turned the shower up full force. The din of the water hitting the aqua-colored plastic shower stall filled the bathroom.

Frank put his mouth close to Joe's ear. "Whisper. I don't think any bugs they might have in here could pick us up."

"This looks bad for Marcie's dad," Joe whispered back. "This operation sure seems to be set up to help crooks skip out."

"Right—and maybe it does even more than that," Frank answered. "It looks too elaborate for just an escape outfit. But we can worry about that later. Right now we have to worry about ourselves. We're in these people's hands, and unless we convince them we're their kind of guys, they're going to start squeezing really hard."

"Yeah, we've got to get our story together," whispered Joe. "I bet that's why they put us in here before the interview, so that if we tried to come up with some story, their bug would pick it up."

"You just figured that out?" whispered Frank.

"Okay, okay," Joe said with more than a trace of annoyance in his whisper. "If you're so smart, how do we explain how a couple of teens like us are loaded with cash and on the run from the law?''

"They were expecting Marcie's dad," whispered Frank. "So I think we should tell them that we were in on his embezzlement scheme."

"Sure, we really look like corporate types," Joe hissed sarcastically.

"Come on, Joe, the answer was sitting right there on Sally's desk."

Joe sat patiently, waiting for his brother to get to the punch line of what he was sure was a joke.

"I'm not kidding. We can claim that we were hackers for hire," Frank told him. "We can say we helped Mr. Miller rig his company's computers so he could get the money out of the country."

"And that when the cops grabbed him, we grabbed our share of the money—" Joe exclaimed.

"And ran," said Frank, finishing his brother's sentence.

Frank turned off the shower and opened the bathroom door. "Hey, that was great, Joe," he shouted into the other room. "You want to take one?"

Joe left the bathroom, then called back toward Frank, "Nah. You took too long. We're going to have our interview in a few minutes. Hope it doesn't drag on—I want to clear out of here fast. I can practically feel Uncle Sam breathing down my neck."

"What could they want to find out?" Frank asked as he came out of the bathroom. "The color of our money should have been enough."

"You can't blame them for checking us out," answered Joe. "In an operation like this, you have to be extra careful."

A minute later Bob opened their door without bothering to knock and beckoned to them to follow.

"Wait a sec," said Frank, and went to pick up the attaché case. "We'd better keep this with us."

Bob shrugged and said impatiently, "Let's go."

He led them down a hall to another room and opened the door. "Here are the two you wanted to see, sir," he said and gestured with his M-16 for the Hardys to go inside.

As they stepped into the room, they heard Bob leave and close the door behind them.

In front of them was a short, squat, balding man with a mustache. He, too, was wearing unmarked fatigues, but his whole presence indicated that he was an officer in whatever kind of force this was. He wasn't sitting behind his desk, but on top of it. One gleaming boot was tapping against the desk front as he looked the Hardys up and down.

"So you are Frank and Joe," he said. It was not a statement but a challenge.

"Right," said Frank.

"And who are you?" asked Joe.

The man smiled. "You can call me Alex."

"Glad to meet you, Alex," said Joe, extending his hand. "Now, how soon can you get us out of here?"

"Ah, you young people, always in such a hurry," Alex said with a sigh, ignoring Joe's outstretched hand. "In fact, you seem quite young to want to take one of our vacations, much less be able to afford it."

Frank had decided that the best way to weather this confrontation was to get this guy on the defensive, so he started talking fast and loud. "Look, I don't see why we have to go through this third-degree. The lady on the phone said there'd be no questions about our past."

Alex smiled. "It wouldn't be good for business to allow any undercover cops to travel along our underground railroad, would it?"

"If you lied on the phone," said Joe, "how can we trust you about anything?"

Alex sighed. "Come on, kid, you might be young, but you can't be that dumb. Who can you trust in this world? Nobody. But if it makes you feel any better, we'll keep our part of the bargain once we clear you. Not out of any sense of honor, but because it's good business. The only way we can keep getting customers is to have them pass the word that we give good value—a new start with a new name in a new place."

Frank pretended to think it over. Then he nodded. "Makes sense. Okay. Marcie Miller is a friend of ours. We met her father at a Halloween party, and he and I got to talking computers. When I told him about how some friends of mine had managed to get into the phone company's computers—"

Joe interrupted, continuing the story. "—he said that such a thing could never happen to his company's computers, that they were state-of-the-art. Later that night we tried it, and they were easy. They had a mainframe set up to take orders over the phone lines, and their security system was a joke. We could have wiped them out."

"But we didn't," interjected Frank. "We just got into the interoffice e-mail—that's electronic mail—system and left Miller a message. The computer wouldn't work for anyone in his company that day until—"

"—they said please," said Joe, laughing out loud.

"Sounds good," said Alex. "But that's nothing to make you start running."

"What came afterward wasn't just fun and games." Frank's face sobered. "Miller told us we were the answer to a businessman's prayer. Working together, with us slipping bogus orders into the computer at night and him moving the money during the day, we really took a bite out of the company. But it looks like he got too greedy and careless. We picked up our last payment just before the cops came to take him away.

When you called, it sounded like the answer to *our* prayers.''

Frank smiled at Alex, then at Joe. When he and his brother were on the same wavelength, it felt as if nothing and nobody could beat them.

"Well, Frank and Joe, you seem to have—" Alex began.

Just then the phone rang. Alex picked it up and listened. Then his eyes narrowed and he said, "Thanks. I'll take care of it."

Without even a glance at the Hardys, he put down his phone, slid off the desk, and opened a drawer. Frank and Joe looked at each other uneasily. Alex's mood had clearly just changed— and it didn't look as if it had changed in their favor. When they looked back at Alex, they saw a .45 in his hand, pointed at them.

"There's one thing you didn't mention, Frank and Joe," he said, a smile spreading slowly across his face. "Maybe you wanted to be modest. But let me tell you, it's a great big thrill to meet the famous Hardys.''

Chapter

5

"WHO'RE THEY?" SAID Joe with a puzzled look.

"Come on, you must have heard of them," said Alex. "They're Fenton Hardy's kids, and they like to play at being detectives like their old man."

"Oh, *those* Hardys," said Frank.

"What do *we* have to do with them?" asked Joe.

The door to the room opened. In walked Bob, his M-16 in one hand and a magazine in the other.

Alex glanced at its cover. "Hmm, *Advanced Computer Abstracts*. So, you're into computers, Frank?"

"What if I am?" said Frank defiantly, then stopped. He suddenly had a sick feeling in the pit of his stomach.

"You're not even going to ask me how I knew

this magazine was yours?'' asked Alex with a gloating smile. ''But I suppose you don't have to. You must realize that your name is on the address label pasted on it. A little careless, Frank. But I guess even the brightest boys make mistakes.''

Frank didn't have an answer. He said feebly, ''You went through our bags while we were down here.''

''Too bad you didn't think of it sooner,'' said Alex.

''What are you going to do with us?'' asked Frank, trying not to look at his brother. He could imagine the look that Joe was giving him.

''Do you have to ask?'' inquired Alex, lowering his gun so it was pointed directly at Frank's heart.

Frank refused to give Alex the satisfaction of seeing him cringe. He kept his face expressionless and braced himself.

''Relax,'' Alex said. ''You have a few more hours—until it gets dark. Then you can take a trip with a couple of our men to a neighboring key. It doesn't have a fine mansion like this one on it. In fact, it doesn't have anything on it but quicksand. We find it very handy. It's as though Mother Nature has given us the perfect disposal machine.''

Then he turned to Bob. ''Take them away.''

''The cellar?'' asked Bob.

''The cellar,'' said Alex. ''You can leave that attaché case here. Money won't do you any good where you're going.''

Bob herded Frank and Joe at gunpoint down the broad stairway to the first floor, then down a much narrower set of steps to an underground passage lined with wooden doors. It was dimly lit by a few light bulbs crudely installed on the ceiling.

"Surprise, huh?" said Bob. "Upstairs was where the owners lived the good life in the old days. Down here is where they used to stick slaves who got too uppity. To teach them a lesson, if you know what I mean."

They reached the end of the passage. Bob made them stand against the damp plaster wall next to the last door.

"Turn your pockets inside out," he instructed sharply. After they had dumped the contents of their pockets onto the floor, he said, "Open that door and get in."

They heard him slide the outside bolt shut.

"Hey, it's pitch black. What about some light?" Joe shouted.

"Get used to the dark. Pretend it's quicksand," Bob said, his voice muffled by the thick door.

Long minutes passed in the silent darkness.

Then Frank heard Joe whisper, "Think he's gone?"

"Probably," Frank whispered back. Then he said in a more normal tone, "I don't think we have to worry about bugs down here."

"I don't know if I should trust your judgment

after your brilliant move with that magazine," Joe said sourly.

"Look, I'm sorry," Frank said. "I was in the middle of an article, so I packed the magazine, intending to finish it and then chuck it. But things happened too fast, and it slipped my mind."

"Which leaves us slipping into quicksand—unless we can find a way out fast," said Joe. "Let's start looking."

A light flashed in his hand.

"Good, you've got your penlight," said Frank. "I knew you'd manage to palm something when that goon made us empty our pockets."

"Yeah," Joe agreed. "What'd you get?"

"This," said Frank, and showed Joe his Swiss army knife.

"We're in business," said Joe.

Frank knelt in front of the door. He examined it, his brow furrowed, concentrating. "Too bad it doesn't have a lock. There's nothing to pick. We have to get at that bolt."

He tested the wood with the tip of the longest blade on his knife.

"We're in luck," he said. "It's old and soft. I could pick it away with my fingernails if I had the time."

"But we don't," said Joe. "Get to work."

"Right," said Frank, and began gaining access to the outside bolt, while Joe provided light with his penlight. With the blade, Frank gouged out wood on the edge of the door; then he used the miniature saw on the Swiss army knife to remove larger chunks. Half an hour later, the metal of the outside bolt was exposed.

"Let's hope they've kept it well oiled," he said, and used the tip of his strongest blade to try to slide the bolt open.

It wouldn't budge.

"Back to work," said Frank, gritting his teeth and cutting at the wood again to widen the opening.

"Hurry it up," urged Joe. "They'll be coming for us any second."

"Thanks for the information," said Frank, wiping away the sweat that beaded his forehead.

Finally the hole looked large enough. "Let's see if I can reach it now," Frank said.

He managed to insert a couple of fingers into the hole and make contact with the metal of the bolt. The surface was rough and rusted. He tried to move it. It wouldn't budge. Finally he gave one last try—and felt it move just a fraction.

"I think I've got it going," he said. "But my fingers are starting to cramp."

"Let me take a crack at it," said Joe.

They exchanged places.

"It's moving, all right, but not much," Joe grunted. "It's really stiff." He withdrew his fingers and shook them to relieve the ache.

They traded places three more times, until Joe finally said, "That does it." He gave the door a push, and it swung open.

"Whew," said Joe. "That's cutting it close."

"I hope not too close," said Frank. "Let's see if we can make it out of here."

Swiftly they moved down the passageway and up the narrow stairs to the first floor. Joe went first, eager to be on the move. But he was cautious enough to stop midway up the stairs, and listen. At the top of the stairs, Joe slowly eased his head around the corner.

"Coast's clear," he whispered over his shoulder. "Let's go."

He raced for an open door. Frank was right on his heels.

They entered a recreation room that held a Ping-Pong table, a pool table, card tables, video games, a giant-screen TV, and soft-drink and snack machines. It, too, was deserted.

"Nice setup," remarked Joe. He went to a soft-drink machine and pressed a button. A plastic cup descended and was filled. "You don't even need change for it," he said, taking a long swallow. "They live pretty well here."

Frank shook his head impatiently. It was good to keep cool in tight spots, but sometimes Joe overdid it.

"We've been lucky so far," Frank said, "but let's get out of here before our luck runs out." Then he exclaimed, "Hey! What the—"

In one lightning motion, Joe had dropped his soda, grabbed a ball from the pool table, and let the ball fly—right at Frank.

There wasn't time for Frank to duck. He barely had a chance to blink as the ball whizzed by his ear. A *clunk* followed, and Frank wheeled around to see a young man in a white uniform toppling like a felled tree. Behind him, in the doorway of the room, another man in white stood with his mouth open in surprise.

The second man didn't get a chance to make a move. Frank connected with a karate chop. The man dropped to the floor, out like a light.

"Not a bad fastball, considering I haven't pitched since August," said Joe, crossing the room to join Frank near the two unconscious men.

"Glad your control was on," said Frank, rubbing the ear the pool ball had almost brushed.

"Trust me," Joe said. "They came through the door too suddenly for me to warn you. I had to move fast."

"And we have to get out of here just as fast," said Frank, but then he stopped himself in mid-movement. "On second thought, let's take time for a quick change."

He bent down to unbutton the clothes of the man at his feet.

"Got you," said Joe, nodding and following Frank's lead.

Minutes later Frank and Joe were clad in white suits that were a little too large and black patent shoes that pinched. Their own clothes had been torn into strips and used to tie and gag the two unconscious men.

"Now, let's find a way out of here," said Frank.

"Easy," said Joe as he raised a large window.

Although it was dark out, a full moon lit the cloudless sky, and the Hardys had to be careful to stay in the shadows of the shrubbery that bordered the side of the mansion.

"What now? The fence around this place is going to be tough to get over. Bet that wire on top is electrified," Joe said as they edged around the mansion toward the rear.

"Quick," Frank whispered suddenly. "Hit the ground!"

Joe had heard the same noise Frank had. They lay on their stomachs, holding their breath, as a group of about twenty men came out of the darkness on an asphalt path fifteen yards from them.

The men passed the spot where Frank and Joe were lying and entered the mansion through a rear door. Frank and Joe lay quietly for a couple more minutes before getting to their feet.

"That explains why the mansion was deserted," whispered Joe. "Most of the help was back there. Wonder what they were doing?"

"As long as they're not hunting us, I'm happy," said Frank. "Whatever they're doing, we have to get moving. In a little while, all those guys *will* be hunting us."

"Let's see how fast you can go," challenged

Joe. "Bet I can still beat you in the two hundred."

"You're on," said Frank, assuming a sprinter's crouch.

The two of them tore over the open lawn behind the mansion toward the asphalt path, and then raced along it.

At the point where the path entered a grove of mangrove trees, Joe came to a halt with a three-yard lead over Frank.

"As slow as ever," Joe panted as Frank stopped beside him.

"Make it five miles, and then see who's ahead," Frank answered automatically, looking behind them. There was still no sign of pursuit. And no fence ahead of them. He looked at the path. No telling where it led.

"Come on," Frank said, and they walked through the grove and emerged from the trees.

"Wow! Look at that," said Joe, stopping to stare at the view that opened out before them.

The path descended to a wharf that jutted out into the sea. Beyond the end of the wharf, the moonlight formed a ghostly ribbon on the smooth water. Ghostly in the moonlight, too, was a sleek white yacht, moored to the wharf.

"Maybe we won't have to swim for it after all," said Joe. "Not with a beauty like that to take us over the water."

"It's worth checking out," said Frank. "I

don't see any sign of life aboard. Maybe we can hijack it."

"Sounds good," said Joe, already moving toward the wharf.

"Careful, this wood is old—watch out for squeaks," whispered Frank when they reached the pier.

"Okay," Joe whispered back. "But there's no danger that I can see. Nobody is—"

A sudden beam of light froze him with his mouth open. Almost as quickly as the light had gone on, it went off.

It took just a second for the Hardys' vision to readjust to the moonlight.

And then they saw the figure of a man dressed in a uniform the same ghostly white as the yacht he was standing on.

But there was nothing ghostly about the man's voice. His shout shattered the stillness.

"Freeze, you two!"

The boys were trapped in the open, the moon hitting them like a spotlight, their moment of freedom over.

Chapter

6

" 'BOUT TIME YOU two showed up," said the man, speaking more softly. "Another five minutes, we would have left without you. They finished loading the ship a good ten minutes ago, and the tide's about to change."

"Uh, we can explain," said Frank quickly, hoping that he or Joe could come up with something fast.

"Save it for when we're below decks," the man said, then squinted at them. "Hey, where's your gear?"

"We sent it down with one of the guys on the loading detail," Frank said. "Didn't he bring it?"

The man gave a snort of disgust. "I can see they sent me a couple of goof-ups for this trip. Nobody brought your gear here—and it's too late to go back to find it. Doesn't matter, anyway.

There's plenty of uniforms on board, real pretty ones. So, you get aboard, too.''

"Okay, okay," said Joe, picking up on this new game. "But isn't this a lot of fuss over us showing up a couple of minutes late?"

"We stick to the rules in this outfit, and don't you forget it," snapped the man.

"Yes, sir. Right, sir," said Frank, and jumped from the wharf onto the deck of the yacht. Behind him came Joe, and then the man in the white uniform.

Joe stumbled over a rope on deck as they headed for a hatchway. "I could have broken my ankle," he complained. "Why don't you turn on some lights?"

"I can see it's going to be real fun teaching you morons the routine," the man said. "What can I expect, though, with last-minute replacements? If only my two regular stewards hadn't eaten those spoiled anchovies." He paused, then said, "Why do you think we don't have any lights? Security. Same reason everything on this trip is done the hard way, like not even using our radio. Nobody sees us, and nobody hears us. I wasn't even supposed to use my flashlight, but I had to check you out."

He opened the hatchway, and bright light shone out from the inside. All the windows and doors must have been blacked out. The man closed the door the moment they were in, then led them down the stairs going below decks.

"In here," said the man, and they entered a large wood-paneled cabin.

Joe uttered a low whistle of approval as he looked around at the luxurious surroundings.

"Yeah, this used to be some millionaire's yacht," said the man. "This cabin is mine, but yours is almost as nice. This ship is good duty. Do your jobs right, and maybe you'll get a permanent assignment."

"Hey, what do we call you?" said Frank.

"My organization name is Sam. What're yours?"

"Well, aboard this ship, I'm Frank," he said.

"And I'm Joe," said Joe.

"Frank. Joe. I'll remember that. And you do, too," said Sam.

"We'll do our best," promised Frank.

"First we have to get you outfitted," said Sam. As he led them out of the cabin and down the passageway, the yacht engine came to life. Under their feet, they felt the ship begin to move.

"We're in our own private world until landfall," said Sam. "This is my fifth trip, and I still haven't gotten used to it. Just like I can't get used to not knowing where we go. We just dock there and stay aboard." He shook his head. "Well, we don't want to know too much in this organization."

Sam took Frank and Joe to a supply room, where an attendant handed them uniforms consisting of black trousers, white shirts, black ties, white formal jackets, an extra pair of black shoes each, and enough socks, underwear, and toilet articles to replace the lost ones in their duffel bags.

Next, Sam took them to their cabin.

"Stow your gear and report to my cabin in ten minutes," he ordered and left them alone.

As they quickly changed into clothes that fit, Frank remarked, "Looks like we're going to be oceangoing waiters."

"I hope we wait on the captain's table," said Joe. "We could find out where we're headed."

"I'd sure like to find out *something*," said Frank. "The deeper we get into this Perfect Getaway outfit, the more questions I have. I mean, this all looks too big and elaborate just to help a handful of rich crooks skip the country—but maybe I'm underestimating the power of money."

Joe finished knotting his tie and looked at himself in the mirror. "How do I look?"

"You can serve me caviar anytime," said Frank. "Come on, let's get back to Sam and find out what we do next."

When they got to Sam's cabin, he looked them over, straightened Joe's tie, and said, "Okay, you two'll do. I know you're not experienced, but you can learn on the job. This trip'll be easy. We just have one passenger aboard. There were supposed to be three, but an hour before we sailed, the reception center called to say that the other two weren't coming.''

"They missed the boat, huh?" Joe asked innocently.

"Maybe they'll catch it on the next run you make," Frank suggested.

"Doubt it," said Sam. "When somebody's crossed off our passenger list, it doesn't mean his trip's canceled. It means *he's* canceled."

"So we've got only this one passenger to take care of," said Joe, to change the subject. "A VIP, huh?"

"All our passengers are VIPs," said Sam, smiling. *"They* think so, anyway—until they find out different."

"So, we give him special attention," said Frank.

"That's right. Extra special attention," said Sam, and his smile grew wider. He opened a drawer and took out a metal object the size of a pack of gum. He handed it to Frank. "I hope you know how to handle *this.*"

Frank did. He looked at it and nodded. "Best miniature camera on the market. I've used this model lots of times." He didn't mention that he had learned to use it from the Network, a top-secret government agency that Joe and he occasionally helped.

"What do we do with the camera?" asked Frank.

"You wait until our passenger leaves his cabin,

and then you go through his stuff and photograph any papers you can find," said Sam.

"What kind of stuff are we looking for?" asked Joe.

Sam shrugged. "Beats me. The orders are to photograph any and all papers, period. I don't ask questions. I never find out *why* I'm doing anything."

"I couldn't care less," Frank said in a bored voice. "All I'm interested in is my pay."

"Right," said Joe. "What you don't know can't hurt you."

"That's a healthy attitude," Sam said. "Come on. I'll introduce you to the passenger. Igor is what we're supposed to call him. Some of these guys come up with really weird names for themselves."

Sam led the way to a door at the end of the passageway and knocked.

"Wait a minute," said a voice from inside. A key was turned in the lock, and the door swung open.

Facing them was a balding, moon-faced, middle-aged man in a rumpled white tropical suit. He looked like a marshmallow, but there was nothing soft about the icy blue eyes behind his rimless glasses. They were sharp and never rested as he looked over the three men at his door.

"No need to lock your door, sir," Sam said genially. "You're among friends here."

"That's for me to decide," the man called Igor

snapped back. His voice was cold and contemptuous, the voice of a man used to giving orders. "What do you want?"

"I want to introduce Frank and Joe here," said Sam, keeping the genial smile on his face with some effort. "They'll be here to serve your every need, twenty-four hours a day. Bring your drinks, launder your clothes, tidy your cabin when you take your meals at the captain's table or go on deck."

"I'm not eating at the captain's table, and I'm not going on deck," Igor said. "I'm staying in here, with my door locked. Although that really won't protect my privacy. I'm sure you've got keys to the lock."

"Of course not," Sam said indignantly. "You requested all the keys when you were brought aboard, and we gave them to you."

"I bet," Igor said, his voice still flat and hard. "Anyway, these two kids can serve me my meals in here—not that I'm expecting to have many. This trip can't take too long, can it?" For the first time, a faint note of uncertainty crept into Igor's voice—an uncertainty born of not being in complete control, possibly for the first time in his life.

"Not long at all," Sam assured him. "Just tonight, then the day after, and the following night. We reach our destination at dawn on the second day."

"I don't suppose I get to find out where that destination is?" said Igor.

"Not right now," said Sam. "You know the rules."

"Yeah, I found them out—too late," said Igor. "I had already gone too far to back out."

"I'm sure you'll find everything to your satisfaction," Sam assured him.

"I'm sure," Igor said sourly. "Okay, you can clear out now. I'll ring when I get hungry. Then you can bring me two chicken sandwiches on white toast with white meat only, and a bottle of diet soda. Got it?"

"Yes, sir," said Frank.

"Anything else?" asked Joe.

"Yeah, my privacy," said Igor. "Clear out until I ring."

As they walked back along the passageway, Frank murmured to Sam, "Well, there goes our chance to do the snooping."

"Are you kidding?" said Sam. "He thinks he's smart. I have something to cut him down to size. Come to my cabin."

In his cabin, Sam pulled out a brown glass vial of pills. He took one out, handed it to Frank, and replaced the jar in his desk drawer.

"When Igor rings for his diet soda, crush this pill and put it in the drink," Sam said. "In about thirty minutes it'll take effect. After that, he'll be out like a light for at least five hours. You'd be able to break his door in and he wouldn't notice."

Then Sam snapped his fingers and said, "Oh,

yeah, I almost forgot.'' He opened another drawer. ''Here's the key to his cabin.''

''So he was right—you did hold out on him,'' said Frank.

''He knows how the game is played,'' said Sam with a shrug. ''The thing is, he doesn't know he's a sure loser, because we have all the cards.''

''I'd almost pity him—if I hadn't met him,'' said Frank.

An hour later Igor rang for his food, and Joe brought the sandwiches and drugged soda.

''Bread's stale,'' Igor complained, testing it with his finger. ''Not much fizz in the soda. And your jacket isn't buttoned up all the way, boy.''

''Sorry, sir,'' said Joe.

''If you think I'm giving you or your sidekick a tip, you're crazy,'' said Igor, and waved him away.

As soon as Joe was back in the passageway, he heard Igor lock the door to his cabin again.

Joe went back to his cabin.

''I wonder what Igor did in the real world, other than bully anyone who crossed his path,'' Joe said to Frank as he climbed up to the upper bunk to rest before they went into action.

Frank looked at his watch. ''We'll give him an hour. By that time he'll be out of the picture, and we can start finding out about him.''

''Real nice of Sam to give us the go-ahead to do some investigating,'' said Joe. ''Makes it easier.''

"It sure does, and we need all the breaks we can get," said Frank. "While you were gone, I went down to the wardroom. Nobody on this crew seems to know anything about anything—or if they do, they're not talking."

"That never stopped you from learning anything before," replied Joe.

Frank thought for a moment. "My guess is that they really don't know anything," he went on. "Whoever set up this operation has fragmented it so that nobody knows the whole picture. From what Sam said, there's no communication between Florida and this ship, and there's no communication between this ship and wherever it docks. Anyone following the trail would hit one dead end after another."

"Look, do me a favor and don't use the expression 'dead end,' " Joe said wryly.

"Okay," said Frank, grinning. "At least we've got one door we can open." He tapped the key to Igor's cabin in the palm of his hand.

Half an hour later they stood in front of that door.

"First we check to make sure the pill has taken effect," whispered Frank.

He knocked loudly on the door.

They waited. No answer.

"Sam was right," said Joe. "Igor must be dead to the world." He grinned. "Oops—there's that dirty word again."

"Anyway, this looks like it'll be safe enough,"

said Frank. He inserted the key, turned it, heard the lock click, and pushed open the door.

Joe went in first.

"It won't hurt to turn on the light," he said, flicking the switch.

The light came on. Igor lay motionless, a huddled lump beneath the blankets.

"Sleeping like a baby." Joe grinned as he moved forward and let Frank enter.

Frank stepped in—and stopped abruptly.

Not because he wanted to. He had no choice.

An arm had snaked out from behind the door and wrapped around his neck, right under his chin, jerking his head back.

At the same moment, something cold and sharp pressed lightly but firmly against his exposed throat, directly over his jugular vein.

Igor's voice hissed in his ear.

"This knife is razor-sharp. The slightest move—and you're dead."

Chapter

7

THE DAY FRANK earned his brown belt, his teacher had given him a piece of advice: "You have attained a certain level of skill, but do not let pride blind you to its limits. There are times when you can do nothing but wait for the moment to strike."

The cold steel of the knife against his throat was all Frank needed to confirm that the slightest move on his part, no matter how fast or smooth, would leave his throat slit wide open.

"Joe, don't move or I'm dead," he said, trying not to disturb the razor-edged blade.

Joe turned slowly, his hands away from his body so Igor could see that he had no weapon.

"Mister, I'm not going to try anything," said Joe.

"I'm glad to know that you two are not entirely

stupid,'' said Igor. "I couldn't be sure. After all, you were idiotic enough to think I'd allow you to drug me so you could search my things.''

"How'd you catch on to it?'' asked Frank. He wanted to keep Igor occupied talking. The more he talked, the better Frank's chances for figuring an escape. He knew that the least increase in pressure on the blade would set off a geyser of blood.

"How do you think?'' Igor said contemptuously. "I haven't survived in this world by trusting people. I've done it by staying one trick ahead of them. Like the way I kept this knife concealed in my umbrella handle when you searched me for weapons. You're like a bunch of children playing a game of double-cross with me. I've played and beaten masters at it.''

Igor chuckled, and the knife jiggled.

"Hey, watch it,'' Frank gasped.

"You mean you don't want to die?'' Igor asked, chuckling louder as Frank winced and Joe watched in helpless horror. "I knew you people would try to squeeze every cent out of me—the money I'm carrying as well as everything that I've hidden around the world.''

"Look, mister,'' said Frank desperately, "we're just hired hands. We get orders and we follow them.''

"I know that,'' said Igor in a bored voice. "And that's the only reason I'm going to let you live. In fact, I'm going to offer you the chance to live very well indeed. What would you two say to a twenty-thousand-dollar bonus? That's twenty thousand dollars apiece.''

"For what?" asked Joe.

Frank cut in quickly. "What does it matter? For twenty grand, I'll do anything you can dream up.''

"That's what I thought you'd say," said Igor with satisfaction. "One good thing about dealing with hired help—you can always hire them yourself if you pay the right price.''

He let Frank go. Frank let out a long breath of relief, touching his throat gingerly, then glanced at his fingertips. No blood.

"Let me show you something, so you'll know you can trust me, and so then I can trust you,'' Igor said. He went to his bunk and pulled away the blanket. Under the blanket was a pile of clothes bundled up to give the illusion of someone sleeping there. He reached under the clothes and pulled out an attaché case.

The attaché case looked familiar.

So did its contents.

Hundred-dollar bills.

The only difference between this case and the one that Frank and Joe had left back in Florida was that this one had many more bills left in it. It was still packed full.

"In case you have any idea of trying to take the whole bundle, forget it," said Igor. "If you do, I'll report you to your superiors. And also forget any idea of shutting my mouth before I can do that. I'm sure your bosses would deal very harshly with anybody who killed their golden goose."

"Boy, you don't trust anybody, do you?" asked Joe, shaking his head.

"Should I?" Igor replied. "The only thing I trust is the power of money. It's gotten me this far, and it will get me my freedom."

"But aren't you worried?" Frank asked. "I mean, if they take that, it's all over for you."

Igor snickered. "You think *this* is money? But I suppose you do. It must look like a lot to guys like you. It's small change. Pocket money."

"Big pockets," commented Joe.

"I'm a big man," said Igor proudly. "I hope you realize that by now."

"We do," said Joe.

"And with the cash you're laying out, we're your boys," said Frank. "What do you want us to do?"

"Tell me where your bosses are taking me, what they plan to do with me," said Igor. Despite his show of bravado, he was unable to hide his uncertainty.

"We'd be glad to, only there's a hitch," said Frank.

"They don't tell the hired help anything," finished Joe.

Igor didn't seem surprised. He nodded. "Makes sense. Whoever runs this outfit is smart.

I'll give him credit for that. He doesn't trust anybody, either. Okay, here's the deal. Sniff around, find out what I want to know, and warn me about any other dirty tricks your bosses plan to pull on me. Do that, and I'll give you each the twenty thousand I promised, plus a bonus." Igor took a handful of bills out of the attaché case. "Here's a thousand apiece to whet your appetites for what's to come if you deliver."

"You've got yourself a deal, mister," said Joe, pocketing the bills.

"Yes, sir, we'll start investigating right away," said Frank. "We'll get back to you as soon as we learn anything."

"Okay, buzz off," said Igor, waving his hand dismissively. "And when they ask you what you found in here, tell them about the attaché case and say there was nothing else you could find. That should satisfy them."

"Thanks, sir," Frank said, still working on buttering him up. "You think of everything."

"That's why I *have* everything," said Igor. He pulled out a cigar and was lighting it with a gold lighter as the Hardys left.

Out in the passageway, Frank turned to Joe. "I don't feel like I'm on a boat. I feel like I'm swimming in the middle of a sea—a sea full of sharks."

"Yeah, and they're all ravenous," said Joe.

"Well, let's go feed Sam the line that Igor

cooked up," said Frank. "Hopefully, it'll keep him from snapping at us."

To their relief, Sam swallowed the story. He shrugged and said, "Well, at least we did our job. They can't blame us if we didn't come up with anything. It won't be the first time."

"What will they do, without the extra information on the passenger?" asked Frank.

"Beats me," said Sam. "They'll pick him up with the rest of our cargo, and that's the last we'll see of him."

"And where will they take him?" Frank persisted.

Sam grimaced wearily. "I already told you, our job is to deliver stuff. After that, we don't have anything to do with it." He looked sharply at Frank. "Hey, what makes you so curious, anyway?"

Joe interrupted hastily. "Frank is naturally nosy. Gets him in trouble, I always say. All *I* want to know is what we're supposed to do now. Do we get some time off?"

"You alternate shifts waiting in the galley," said Sam. "One of you has to be on call in case Igor rings. The other can sack out in the cabin, or play cards or whatever in the rec room. But watch out for the off-limits sign. It's not for decoration. On this ship, if you break a rule, you don't just say goodbye to your job. You say goodbye, period."

"Got you," said Frank.

"No problem," said Joe.

"Me, I'm going to get some shut-eye," said Sam, stretching and yawning. "Don't wake me unless there's an emergency. There won't be much time to sleep. We'll be unloading in less than twenty-four hours, and then clearing out in a hurry."

Frank glanced at his watch in surprise. "I didn't realize it was day already. With everything blacked out, I can't tell night from day."

"Yeah, it is weird, huh," Sam agreed as he went to lie down in his bunk. "The bosses love to keep us all in the dark."

By the time Frank and Joe reached the door, Sam was already snoring. Frank closed the door softly, then said, "I'll take first shift in the galley. I'll try to find out if the cook knows anything. The way this operation is set up, I don't have much hope, though."

"I'll do some nosing around myself," said Joe.

"Hey, be careful," said Frank.

"Sure, you know me," said Joe.

"That's the trouble," Frank said with a grimace.

Joe slapped Frank on the shoulder and watched him head for the galley. Then Joe made a beeline for the one thing he always found irresistible—an off-limits sign.

Sam had made sure to point it out to the Hardys on their fast tour of the ship. But even if he hadn't, there was no way to miss it. Posted right next to a stairway, it was three feet by three feet with bright red letters: CAUTION. OFF-LIMITS. NO UNAUTHORIZED PERSONNEL PAST THIS POINT. ALL VIOLATORS PUNISHED SEVERELY! The word "severely" was underlined in black.

Joe glanced quickly up and down the passageway to make sure nobody was coming, then darted down the stairway.

He descended into a dimly lit cargo hold. Several dozen unmarked wooden crates filled it. He shone his penlight on a few. As Joe walked around the cases, the smell of Cosmoline, the sweet, sticky grease that arms manufacturers use to pack their wares, filled his nostrils. The hold smelled like the National Guard Armory back in Bayport.

I have an idea what these things hold, he thought as he took out the Swiss army knife that had come with his steward's uniform. He pried open a crate and reached inside.

Yuck, he thought, and pulled back his hand. His fingers were covered with the dark grease that he had been smelling.

Well, my hands can't get any greasier, he decided, and pulled the partially opened lid wider so that he could shove in both hands. He took a firm grip on the grease-covered metal he felt and pulled it out. He was holding a submachine gun. He quickly replaced the weapon and put the lid back on the crate, then wiped his hands on a rag. He looked around the hold at the other crates.

"There must be a whole arsenal down here," he muttered. As he looked around one last time, he noticed a group of fiberglass and steel boxes sitting in one corner of the hold.

What else do they need? he wondered as he moved to open the top box. There, nestled in a foam cradle, was a machine that so surprised Joe that it took him one long moment to recognize what it was—a lie detector.

"Guns and gadgets! What *is* going on here?" he whispered. "I've got to tell F—"

Just then he heard a sound. He squeezed himself into a perfect hiding place made by a gap between two crates.

He could just make out the high-pitched voices of two men who seemed to be stationary. They were clearly arguing about something.

Joe carefully edged his way between the crates toward the voices. He rounded the last crate in the row and found himself facing a steel door. The door was open a crack, and the voices were coming from inside.

"I'm starving," said one voice. "I'm going upstairs to get some chow."

"You know the orders," said a second voice. "No mingling with the crew. We're supposed to keep out of sight until we get off-loaded tomorrow."

"Just my luck to be stuck with a by-the-book partner," said the first man.

"I'm making the same money you are," said the second. "And I'm not going to risk losing it."

"Well, there's no way *I'm* going to wait one minute more to get fed," retorted the first man. He pulled open the door and stepped out.

It happened too suddenly for Joe to hide. The man and Joe stared each other in the eye.

Joe opened his mouth, searching for some kind of explanation. But the man wasn't waiting for an explanation. Before Joe could blink, the guy launched a savage left hook.

Before the fist connected with his jaw, all Joe had time to do was form a single word in his mind. Caught! he thought, and then the punch sent him spinning into a pitch-black night streaked with multicolored shooting stars of pain.

Chapter

8

JOE WAS DOWN but not out. Even with his mind teetering on the brink of consciousness, his body reacted instinctively. The moment he hit the floor, he started rolling, away from the fist that had sent him heading toward dreamland. At the same time, Joe shook his head, trying to clear away the cobwebs.

The next couple of seconds seemed like hours as he stopped rolling, tensed his legs to get to his feet, and forced his eyes to open, although that was the last thing he wanted to do.

Through a blur, he saw that the man had followed him. What Joe could see all too clearly, but couldn't do anything about, was the tip of the man's boot heading straight toward his chin.

It never made it.

There was a clang so loud that for an instant

Joe thought someone was pounding a gong inside his head. Then there was a series of crashing noises, like the sound of dishes breaking.

On his hands and knees, still dazed, Joe watched helplessly as Frank lifted the steel tray and brought it down on the back of the man's head again. Then he whirled around to face the other man, who was coming out of the room.

He swung the tray in a level arc so that the edge caught the second man in the stomach. Then, as the man doubled over, Frank lifted the tray up and—crack—it hit the bottom of the man's chin, snapping his head back. He toppled backward, hit a wall, and crumpled to the floor.

Frank gave both fallen men a glance to make sure they were unconscious. Then he went to Joe, who was still trying to struggle to his feet.

"You okay?" he asked, helping Joe up.

Joe touched his chin gingerly and winced slightly. "Bruised but nothing broken," he said. "Thanks for showing up in time. The tip of that guy's boot could have done a lot more damage than his fist. How did you get here, anyway?"

"Bit of luck," said Frank. "While I was sitting around in the galley, the cook told me to rouse Sam. Seems it was Sam's job to deliver chow to these guys down here. Nobody else was supposed to talk to them. But when I told the cook that Sam was sacked out and would get real mad if I woke him up, the cook decided it wouldn't hurt for me to bring the food down, if I did it real fast and kept my mouth shut. Needless to say, I was glad to oblige. It seemed like a terrific chance to find out more about what's happening. I didn't realize it'd also be a chance to get you out of a jam."

Joe couldn't argue. "No risks, no rewards," he said weakly. "And for this risk, I discovered that this hold is filled with crates of weapons and some really weird stuff. I thought we were dealing with arms smugglers until I found a lie detector and a bunch of other electronic equipment over in the corner. Now I don't know what's going on here."

"Neither do I," said Frank. "We keep uncovering more questions than answers."

"I did learn one thing," Joe replied. "I overheard these two guys talking. Seems they've taken jobs with whoever is running this show. From what they said, they're supposed to be picked up with the cargo."

"Hey, that *is* good," said Frank, looking at the two unconscious men with new interest. "Come on, let's tie them up fast, before they come to. Then we can find out what they know."

They took some rope off one of the crates and used it to tie up the men. But by the time they had tied the last knots and were waiting for the men to regain consciousness, Frank was having second thoughts about their chances of getting information.

"I'll bet they don't know any more than anybody else," he said. "Every part of this operation is kept separate from every other part. These guys wouldn't be told anything until they moved on to the next part of the operation."

"Right," said Joe. "If we want to find out what's going on and where, we'll have to do it by ourselves."

"Too bad we're not in these guys' shoes," said Frank. Then he paused, looking at the pair with new interest.

Joe was quiet, too, as he looked at them. Then he asked, "Are you thinking what I am?"

"Probably," said Frank. "The idea is crazy enough."

"Crazy enough to work," Joe said. "These guys are about our sizes."

"And their hair coloring is close to ours, too," said Frank, warming to the idea. "One's got brown hair like mine; the other is blond like you. We could pass for them if we managed to dodge the crew members who've seen us already."

"Should have known you'd be ready to go for it," Joe said, grinning. This was more like it, he thought. He and Frank were swinging into action. It was time to stop running from danger, time to launch an attack.

Meanwhile, Frank was thinking out loud.

"Getaway's policy of keeping its employees in the dark is its strength, but also its weakness," he said. "It's impossible to trace them from Florida to wherever headquarters is. But on the other hand, each time we get past one of the roadblocks they've set up, nobody can chase us or call ahead to warn anybody about us. Because nobody knows where we're going after we leave their particular operation.''

"So the same shield that protects the higher-ups protects us, too," said Joe, grinning.

"Not exactly," said Frank. "Sooner or later, we're going to run into somebody who knows enough of what's going on to know that we don't belong here. And we are a long way from any sort of backup. When we run out of places to go, we have a problem. A *real* problem.''

"So, we make sure that we always have an escape route open," said Joe, shrugging. "As long as we keep moving, I think we're in good shape.''

"I hope so," said Frank, then turned back to the problem at hand. "First thing we have to do is see Igor.''

"Why?" asked Joe. "You don't trust him, do you?''

"No," said Frank. "But we have to make sure he doesn't give us away when he sees us. He's going to be picked up at the same time as the cargo and us.''

Frank and Joe hauled the two limp men into the back room and made sure the ropes that bound them were secure. Then they put gags in the men's mouths. They planned to come back when the ship neared the shore, and put on the men's khakis.

Then they went to Igor's cabin.

He was glad to see them.

"What did you find out?" he asked. "Remember, no info, no more money."

"Sorry, pal," said Joe, shrugging. "Nobody knows anything."

"I should have known," said Igor with disgust. "I was dumb to give you two a penny. In fact, I want my money back."

"What are you going to do if we don't hand it over?" Joe sneered, acting the part of a young thug. "You figure on taking it from us?"

"I won't have to," said Igor smugly. "I'll simply report that someone stole two thousand dollars from me, and your superiors will take it from you for me."

"You're a real nice guy, aren't you," said Joe, waving a clenched fist in front of Igor's eyes. "I've got half a mind to—"

Frank cut in on his tirade. "Cool it, Joe. Use that half a mind of yours. Igor's got a lot more than two thousand dollars for us if we treat him right."

Frank turned to the balding businessman and apologized. "Don't let my buddy bother you. We know that we didn't come up with much, but we think we can give you your money's worth. Actually, we can do something that's worth a lot more than the twenty thousand that you offered us."

"So far we agree on one thing—neither of you

has earned the thousand I gave you," Igor said angrily. "What do you propose to do to earn any more of my money?"

"We made a deal with two guys we ran into," said Frank. "They're new recruits who are going to the same place you are. We gave them a thousand apiece to let us go in their places. That way, we'll be able to look out for you, keep you posted, and keep you protected."

"For a price," said Joe in a harsh voice. "A bigger one than you offered. We had to pay off those two guys, and we're taking more risks. We want our payoff doubled."

"Highway robbery," snapped Igor.

"Take it or leave it," said Frank.

Igor looked at their faces. Both of them kept their expressions flat and cold. Igor shrugged. "Okay. I'll pay. You can't blame me for wanting to negotiate a bit, though. Lifetime habits are hard to break."

He gave them a big, friendly smile that was about as convincing as the sun rising in the west.

"Sure," said Frank, giving him the same kind of smile in return. "No hard feelings."

"So long as we get the cash," said Joe, concluding the negotiations.

After they left Igor's cabin, Frank said, "That worked fine. The one way to convince him we're on the up-and-up was to convince him we'd do anything for money. That's the only thing he believes in."

75

Then he added, "I'm heading back to the galley before they come looking for me. We don't want anybody wandering down in the hold and spotting those two guys we tied up. We'll make the clothing switch as close to landfall as we can. Cut down our chances of being caught."

"Right," said Joe. "I'll get some sleep and then relieve you. Wake me when you get tired."

They parted in the passageway, and Joe went to their cabin.

He hadn't realized how tired he was until he saw his bunk. He didn't bother taking off all his clothes, just his white steward's jacket and his black shoes. He lay down in the bunk and was sound asleep as soon as his head hit the pillow.

His sleep was deep—so deep that even when he started dreaming he knew it was all a dream, as if he were standing a safe distance outside of himself, so that nothing could really hurt him.

He saw Jeeves, the chauffeur, pointing a gun at him and saying in his British accent, "Better start running now, sir, better start running fast, faster than my bullets."

He saw himself running, stumbling over sand that kept slipping beneath his feet, so that he didn't go forward but just kept digging himself deeper and deeper into a hole.

Finally he was at the bottom of the hole, looking up at the light of the sky above. And then the light was blotted out by a face that belonged to

Alex, the man who had grilled him and Frank at the Florida mansion.

Alex was smiling a sneering, triumphant smile and saying, "I didn't have to put you in quicksand, after all. You've dug your own grave."

Then Alex began kicking sand down onto Joe's upturned face, and Joe heard himself shouting desperately, "Frank, come on, time to get going! Move it!"

Then Alex's face was gone, and there was Frank's, close to him, right above him.

"Frank, I knew you'd show up. You know I'd do the same for you," Joe said in relief. Then he saw that Frank's face wasn't smiling, but tight-lipped and grim.

And he suddenly realized that Frank's hand was on his shoulder, shaking him.

Shaking him awake.

He sat up in bed and looked groggily past Frank, and saw Sam standing in the doorway with a gun in his hand and a look of vicious anger on his face.

And Joe knew that this was no dream.

It was a nightmare made real.

Chapter

9

"GET ON YOUR feet—*fast,*" said Sam in a snarl that shredded the last doubts Joe had that he was awake and that this was all real.

Joe sat up, swung himself down out of his bunk, and stood beside Frank. He needed no prompting to follow Frank's lead when his brother put both hands in the air.

"What happened?" he asked.

"I was in the galley about half an hour ago when Sam rang and told me to bring him some coffee. When I did, he shoved this gun in my face and told me to lead him to you. I didn't have any choice."

"And now you don't have any chance," said Sam. "You two kids got your nerve, trying to play me for a sucker."

"How'd you find out?" asked Joe.

"How do you think?" said Sam. "When I woke up from my little nap, I remembered I was supposed to bring those guys down in the hold their chow. I went to the galley and found out that Frank had already gone. After I chewed out the cook for breaking the off-limits rule, I went down to make sure Frank kept his mouth shut about what was down there. I guess you know what I found."

"I guess I do," said Joe, his stomach sinking.

"And I guess you know what's going to happen to you now," said Sam.

"I really don't want to find out," said Joe, searching desperately for a way out of this jam. He hoped Frank was doing the same.

Frank shrugged, apparently unconcerned, and said, "I suppose our luck had to run out sometime. You have to admit, though, we got pretty far."

"And you're going to keep going far—all the way to the bottom of the sea," said Sam.

"What're you going to do?" asked Frank. "Make us walk the plank?"

"No, that would be too public," said Sam. "You won't leave this room alive. After I shoot you two, the only ones who will notice are the fish when you sink past them in the water."

"Gee," said Frank, "I hate to make you miss any sleep while you're waiting for a chance to toss us over the side undetected. You've had so little rest since we left port."

"Yeah, well, I can sleep all the way back to Florida on the return trip. Not that I wouldn't mind a little sack-time right now, but—" Sam paused to give a big yawn. "Yeah, wouldn't mind a"—he gave another yawn—"nap. Funny, I feel kind of—" He shook his head, as if trying to clear it.

"Maybe you should sit down," Frank suggested. "You look tired. *Really* tired."

"Maybe I will," said Sam, sitting down. "But don't you two get any—" Another yawn. "Remember, I still got this—" And as his eyes closed and his head slumped forward, the gun dropped from his fingers and clattered to the floor.

"Whew," said Frank with relief. "Thought that stuff would never get to work."

"Stuff?" said Joe. "What stuff? What happened?"

"On my way back to the galley, I figured I'd look in on Sam to make sure he was still napping," said Frank. "He was gone, so I decided to use the opportunity to lift some sleeping pills from that bottle he put back in his drawer. I figured we could use them to knock him out before we jumped ship, since he was the only one who might stop us. Then, when I got back to the galley and he rang for coffee, I saw my chance to knock him out of action. I put in a triple dose. Luckily, he gulped down the coffee while he was questioning me back in his cabin. From then on,

I had to hold my breath and pray he'd drop off before he knocked us off.''

"Think he'll sleep until we're off the ship and beyond his reach?" said Joe, looking down at Sam, who had slipped off the chair and lay snoring on the floor with a peaceful smile on his face.

"From what he said about those pills, we stand a good chance," said Frank. He stooped down to pick up Sam's gun and concealed it in his shirt. "Come on, help me lug Sam back to his cabin. From what the cook said, he's known for liking lots of shut-eye. We have to hope that nobody thinks it too strange if he stays sacked out.''

As they hauled Sam down the passageway, they passed a crewman, who glanced at them curiously.

"Sam here had a few too many," Joe told him. "I warned him, but he wouldn't listen.''

"Yeah," said Frank. "He's out like a light, and he weighs a ton. Wouldn't be surprised if he sleeps right through the unloading. Leave us to do his work for him.''

"It wouldn't be the first time Sam pulled a stunt like that," said the crewman. "The guy drinks like a fish and sleeps like a log." The man looked at Sam, who by now was snoring loudly. He shook his head with disgust and continued on his way.

"This may actually work," said Joe as they deposited Sam onto his bunk.

"Don't my plans always work?" Frank replied with a grin.

"I won't answer that," said Joe. "I want to stay optimistic."

"You've got to keep the faith," chided Frank. "Now, let's go after those two guys in the hold. They should still be where we found them, since they're not supposed to show themselves to the crew."

Again Frank was on target. When he knocked on the door of the cabin in the cargo hold, a voice answered from within, "Who's there?"

"Sam," Frank answered.

The door swung open, and a minute later the two men were backed up against a wall, their hands over their heads, their eyes fixed on the gun in Frank's hand.

Upon questioning, they gave their names as Dave and Mike.

Frank could have gotten their last names, too—the fear in their eyes told him that. But their last names weren't what he was interested in. He wanted to find out just one thing.

"Does either of you know where you're supposed to be going?" he demanded in a harsh voice. "Don't play games. Tell me the truth. I get very upset when people lie to me."

"Hey, guys, cool it," Dave said hurriedly. "No sweat. I'll tell you anything I can."

"Me, too," Mike seconded. "I'm just in this

for the money. And there's no amount of money worth dying for."

"Good to see that both of you are using your heads," said Frank. "Now, talk."

"Trouble is," said Dave, "there's not much I can tell you. All I know is I answered an ad for adventurers only, and I was promised really good pay for two years' work if I followed orders and didn't ask any questions."

"Same with me," said Mike. "The guy who hired me wouldn't tell me where I was going. I was just supposed to be picked up on a beach near Miami, which I was, by limo, along with Dave here. We couldn't even see out the limo windows. Next thing we knew, we were being grilled by some guy in a big old house, and then we were stuck down here and told to stay here until we were off-loaded. Honest, we're in the dark about this whole deal."

"You've got to believe us," pleaded Dave, staring at the revolver in Frank's hand, sweat beading his forehead.

"I don't know why I should, but I do," Frank said in a grudging voice.

"You guys are lucky we're such trusting souls," said Joe, silently agreeing with his brother that the guys' stories made sense. "But don't push your luck. One wrong move, and we'll turn out your lights for good."

"Yes, sir," said Mike.

"Anything you say," said Dave.

They were as good as their word. Frank and Joe quickly traded clothes with them, then tied them up and gagged them once again.

"Luckily, they don't know where we're going, so they can't help anyone find us," said Joe.

Frank nodded, then stifled a yawn. "Maybe we ought to join Sam in dreamland for a couple of hours. There's nothing to do now but wait for landfall at dawn."

Joe found himself yawning, too. "Guess you're right."

"I'll set the alarm on Mike's watch to wake us at five," said Frank.

"Hope there are no rude awakenings before that," said Joe soberly, climbing up into the upper bunk in Dave and Mike's quarters. Frank lay down in the lower one.

It seemed like only minutes before the beeping of the watch woke them. They had barely washed up in the lavatory connected with the cabin when they heard the sound of men and machinery outside in the hold.

"Let's get out of here before somebody comes and sees these two tied up," said Frank. He started to hide the gun in his shirt again, then stopped and shook his head. He thrust it under the mattress of the bottom bunk. "We're better off without this. Dad always says that carrying a gun usually gets you into more trouble than it gets you out of. What we need is brainpower, not firepower."

"Right," agreed Joe. "Anyway, we promised Dad we'd leave guns alone unless it was life or death." Then he added, smacking his fist in his palm, "Though muscle power can come in handy, and Dad can't complain about that."

"Spoken like a true muscle-head," Frank said, then ducked a mock punch that Joe threw at him. Then sounds outside the cabin jerked them back to reality. This was no time for joking. It was time to save their skins.

Frank opened the door and looked out cautiously. Crewmen were loading the crates in the hold onto wooden pallets, attaching the pallets to cables descending from the open cargo hatch above, and standing aside to watch them being lifted up and away.

"Wonder where the stuff is going?" Frank muttered, leaving the cabin and signaling to Joe that it was safe to follow. Everyone was too busy to notice them.

"We'll find out quickly enough," said Joe. "Let's get up on deck fast, before the activity slows down."

Minutes later they stood on deck in the faint early-morning light. The yacht was anchored close to shore in a natural deep-water cove. On the shore, a tall crane was lifting the loaded pallets out of the hold and depositing them on the ground. There, men driving forklifts were picking up the pallets and carrying them into an opening in a thick tropical forest.

"I can see why they picked this time of day to unload," said Frank. "There's enough light to see, but it's still dim enough for them to avoid easy detection. Their security never lets up."

Just then a voice from behind made them wheel around. "Mike? Dave? About time you two showed up."

A man in crisply pressed khakis with a gleaming leather belt around his waist stood facing them. He was slapping his hand impatiently against his thigh below a holster that hung from his belt. The expression on his face told Frank and Joe that his eyes, invisible behind dark aviator sunglasses, were glaring at them. Although he wore no sign of rank, it was clear who was in command.

Both Hardys snapped to attention.

"Sorry, sir," Frank said.

"The guy on the ship was late waking us," said Joe.

"I haven't got time to listen to your excuses," the man said. "Which of you is which?"

"Mike here," said Frank.

"Dave here," said Joe.

"Okay," the man said. "Continue using first names only, but now you're Mike Seven, and you're Dave Eleven, to avoid confusion among personnel. Got it?"

"Yes, sir," Frank and Joe responded in unison.

"Now, lift your arms above your heads, both of you," the officer ordered.

Frank and Joe instantly obeyed, and the officer quickly frisked them.

"Good," he said, stepping back and indicating that they could lower their hands. "Some recruits disregard instructions and arrive armed, which is bad news for everybody. Some guys are too dumb to live."

"Not us, sir," said Frank fervently.

"We know how to obey orders," Joe seconded.

"That's a very healthy attitude—healthy for you," said the commander. "Now, let's move it."

He led the way off the yacht onto the gangway that stretched between the ship and shore. As soon as they were on land, the commander nodded to a crew of men in nearly identical khakis, who started unhooking the gangway, getting ready to wheel it away.

The commander marched Frank and Joe toward the opening in the forest where the cargo was being taken. The light was still too dim for them to see what was in the jungle shadows.

Only when they reached the edge of the forest could they see what was waiting for them.

Waiting among the trees was a train—a small diesel locomotive with a passenger car and a string of five boxcars.

"Put your eyes back in your heads—it's real," snapped the man. "All aboard."

Frank and Joe climbed into the passenger car. It was the kind seen in old black-and-white

European movies, with a passageway running beside several separate compartments. Each compartment contained seating for six, three seats facing three more.

As they passed the first compartment, they saw Igor sitting inside, flanked by stone-faced men in khaki. He was trying to look at ease, but sweat was pouring down his face.

"You two are in luck," the commander said. "You get a compartment all to yourselves. There aren't many passengers this trip. Make yourselves comfortable. See you in a couple of hours when we reach the ranch. Your orientation starts there."

Frank and Joe sat facing each other on the faded blue plush seats of the compartment. Both peered out the window. All they could see was a thick rain forest of very tall trees.

Frank slid open the window, stuck his head out, and looked upward. After several moments, he pulled his head in again. "Pretty clever. They've extended nets between the tops of the trees on both sides of the tracks and covered the nets with foliage. Looks like they've laced the top branches together, too. They've made sure that nobody can spot the tracks from above. It's as if we're in a tunnel."

There was a gentle lurch, and the train started moving.

"Remember how Alex mentioned their underground railway, Joe? I read about the original one—the operation that helped runaway slaves escape from the South before the Civil War," Frank said. "Guess you could call this the *underworld* railway."

"Yeah, the Crime Rail Express," said Joe. "Just wish I knew where it was heading."

Frank nodded in agreement as he squinted out the window, but he could see less and less as the light at the opening of the tunnel faded behind them. The train sped on, deeper and deeper into the darkness of the unknown.

Chapter

10

"BET YOU ALL are a mite curious about this railway," said the tall man in a cowboy hat and the now-familiar khakis. He had met them as they got off the train at a distant corner of the ranch.

But even if the Hardys had not been told, they would have been able to guess that this man, introduced only as "Chief," was in absolute control of this huge highland ranch at the edge of the jungle.

"Yes, Chief," Frank and Joe answered as they had been instructed to do.

"Real interesting story, that railway," said the man. He was smiling with his mouth, but his eyes stayed hard. He kept Frank and Joe standing at stiff attention while he paced in front of them, the jungle a backdrop. He was making sure they knew who was in charge there. "It was built by an

American about ninety years ago. He saw those little countries here in Central America all split by civil wars and fighting with each other, and he figured that a good, enterprising American could come down here and take charge. Carve out his territory, just like a man used to be able to do in the West before all the land got settled. Well, this fellow came down here and did just that. Built this ranch, declared it an independent country with himself as president for life, ran a railroad to the sea, and had himself sitting pretty. Trouble was, the folks down here got their act together and put this fellow in front of a firing squad, and that was that. The ranch, his little kingdom, went to seed, and the railway tracks were overgrown by jungle—until I came along. You might say I'm following in that fellow's footsteps, except I'm not making his mistakes. You see, I know how to protect myself. I know what to protect myself with. And you boys know what that is?"

He looked at Frank and Joe, demanding an answer.

"Guns?" said Joe.

"Sure, I got them," said the chief. "But I'm talking about something more powerful. The most powerful thing in the world."

"You don't mean atomic weapons?" said Frank, trying not to shudder.

"Nah, don't need them with what I've got, though I expect I could get some if I wanted to," the chief said, his grin widening. "What I'm talking about is money. Money and information. That's all I need.''

Frank and Joe exchanged a quick glance. Once again, just when they thought they'd found the answer to some of their questions, they'd discovered that all they had was a new set of questions.

"Yes, sir, money nearly does it all,'' the chief went on. "But I don't have to tell you two that. Money is what got you down here, right?''

"Yes, Chief,'' Frank and Joe answered.

"But I've got news for you,'' the chief went on. "All the money in the world can't get you out of here, and you remember that. Nobody leaves here before I say they can. Nobody leaves here alive, that is. You got that?''

"Yes, Chief,'' the Hardys responded again.

"Glad you got the message,'' said the chief. "Now, you boys follow orders, keep your noses clean, and maybe when your two years are up I'll figure I can trust you and let you go home. But remember—one little foul-up and you two ain't going nowhere, except six feet under the ground.''

"Yes, Chief,'' said the Hardys, beginning to feel like broken records.

"Okay, you can go now,'' the chief said. "Dimitri!'' he called. "Assign these boys their duties.'' He turned and strode away.

Dimitri, the man who had ridden on the train with them, walked over and joined them.

"Did the chief give you his orientation speech?" Dimitri asked.

"Yeah, if that's what you call it," said Joe.

"That's what I call it," Dimitri said in a voice that made it clear that he didn't like wisecracking. Then he commanded, "Come with me. Time to get that cargo off the train."

He drove Frank and Joe in a jeep to the boxcars, where men were loading the weapon crates onto a large flatbed track.

"Start sweating," he told the Hardys, and they joined the others working in the broiling heat. Even there in the highlands, on a plateau above the rain forest, it was clear that this was Central America. They could feel the sun directly overhead, beating straight down on their backs as they worked.

When all the crates had been loaded, Frank and Joe climbed into the back of the truck with the other men, and the truck started rolling. It bounced along a dirt road that cut through lush grassland dotted with herds of cattle until it reached the bank of a wide, slow-moving river.

Dimitri climbed out of the front of the truck and told the men to climb down from the back. He pulled a walkie-talkie and snapped it on. Frank and Joe, standing close to him, could hear him speaking in Spanish.

After he had finished, he said, "Okay, men, we wait here. Shouldn't take long for them to cross over."

Joe peered toward the other side of the river. Jungle grew down to the opposite bank.

"Who are we expecting?" he asked.

"Bandits. Guerrillas. Freedom fighters. Call them whatever you want," said Dimitri with a shrug. "They're our first line of defense and the main reason that no prisoner ever gets very far. We keep them supplied with arms and ammunition, and they guard our perimeter. What they do with the guns the rest of the time is their own business."

Two large, flat-bottomed boats were crossing the river, propelled by loudly chugging engines. Aboard them were bearded men in jungle camouflage uniforms.

When they had reached the near bank, Dimitri turned to his men. "Load the stuff aboard."

Frank and Joe teamed up to haul crates aboard the boats. They were able to talk in whispers as they worked.

"They've sure got this place sewn up tight," muttered Frank, grunting as he bent to lift one end of a heavy crate. "Thick jungle all around, bandits hiding behind trees."

"Kind of a funny setup for the Perfect Getaway," Joe agreed as he lifted the crate's other end. "I mean, what do they need a ranch for? A couple of plastic surgeons and an acting coach ought to be enough." The two boys carefully boarded the first boat, lugging the crate between them, and set it down at the feet of a surly-looking bandit. Keeping silent until they were once again on land, they continued their conversation as they loaded several more crates.

"Something smells rotten here," Joe murmured. "And I don't think it's the river water, either."

"What has me worried is how *we'll* manage to get out of here," Frank answered. "The only way I can think of is to somehow get word to Dad or the Gray Man."

Joe frowned. The Gray Man was the Hardys' contact in a top-secret American intelligence operation and a hard man to get hold of. They'd helped the operation out more than once. But the only way they knew of to contact him was via modem from Frank's home computer. They were a long way from that computer now.

"Well, it's only a two-year enlistment," Joe joked lamely as they loaded the last crate onto the boat. "It'll fly before we know it."

"Yeah, sure," Frank muttered.

After the loading was finished and the boats were heading back across the river, Dimitri told Frank and Joe to climb into his jeep while he sent the other men back to the truck.

Dimitri sat in back with the Hardys and told his driver, "We're making a tour of the ranch so our new men here understand the layout. You know, the standard orientation tour."

The man said, "Yes, sir," and started the jeep back over the dirt road.

Again they passed the grazing cattle, and Dimitri explained, "That's where we get our beef. Not to mention that the chief likes to play cowboy. He rides a horse and lassos steer, brands them, that kind of stuff." Dimitri smiled, as if at a private joke. "It's one of his favorite hobbies."

The jeep turned onto another dirt road, and they drove to where the grassland turned into fields of corn and grain and vegetables.

"This is where we get the rest of our food," Dimitri explained. "The chief has made this ranch practically self-supporting."

"How many people live here?" Frank asked.

"Oh, plenty." Dimitri gazed off into the distance. "And they stay a long time."

"Is it expensive?" Joe exchanged glances with Frank. They needed information, but weren't sure how far they could push Dimitri without his getting suspicious. At the moment, he seemed not to notice how curious these two young recruits were.

"You never saw anything so expensive in your life," he bragged. "See that?" He pointed toward a large complex that had just become visible in the distance, at the edge of the surrounding jungle. "That's the ranch house. Only the truly elite can afford to stay there. A suite in the big house costs fifty thousand a month, and that's just for a room and continental breakfast, no more. You pay for extras. A good meal costs a thousand bucks. Clean sheets, five hundred. Laundry and dry cleaning, a grand a week.''

''Why would anyone pay that much?'' Frank asked incredulously. ''How ritzy can the place be?''

''Oh, it's ritzy, all right. But that's not why people stay. See, the catch is, it costs five million dollars in cash to check *out*.''

''Five m—'' Frank started to say, but Joe stopped him with a nudge in the ribs and a gesture toward the cornfield to one side of them. There, a group of men and women chopped wearily at some weeds. A man in khakis with a rifle in the crook of his arm was overseeing them. As the jeep drew closer, Frank and Joe could see that, while most of the workers were probably locals, a few among them were middle-aged, paunchy, sunburned, and obviously not accustomed to fieldwork. All wore ragged clothing and frayed straw hats that did little to keep out the burning sun as they hacked methodically at the soil. They were clearly bone-weary.

Suddenly there was a small commotion. One of the workers had fallen to the ground and lay still, face down. The other workers gathered around him.

Dimitri told his driver to head over to the scene of the trouble so that he could check it out. When the jeep arrived, Dimitri climbed out, followed by Frank and Joe.

By now the man who had collapsed was being

helped to his feet by fellow workers, while the guard looked on in a bored way.

Frank and Joe could see that the man was in late middle-age, with a stubble of beard on his hollowed-out cheeks and dark circles of fatigue under his watery blue eyes.

Something stirred in Frank's memory. He was sure he had seen that face before. But he couldn't remember where.

Dimitri, though, knew who the man was. "Hans? Causing trouble again? Won't you ever learn?"

Something inside the man seemed to snap. He straightened up, his nostrils flared with anger, his eyes ablaze. For a moment he was no longer a cowering field-worker. His voice was the voice of someone who was used to being in command. "Stop with this 'Hans' nonsense! I am sick of these silly games you play here. Call me by my right name, at least. Karl, Karl Ross. A man who could buy and sell you a million times over!"

A shiver ran through Frank. Karl Ross. Now he remembered where he had seen that face: on the front page of the newspaper when the financier had mysteriously disappeared, just before he was to be indicted for stealing millions in the stock market.

Dimitri's voice was laced with sarcasm as he said, "Hans, maybe that was true once, but you're broke now. And the ranch is your home. Don't you like it here? Maybe you should try to escape again. Next time you get lost in the jungle, the guard might not find you and bring you back. You might get away and keep going until the jaguars or snakes or alligators finish you off. Or you could cross the river and have our friends over there nab you.''

Dimitri turned to Frank and Joe. ''I heard that Hans here was a real smart operator on the outside. But he's acted real dumb around here. After he went broke, he had a real nice job in the ranch kitchen washing dishes. But he gave it all up when he tried to get away. Guess he thought escaping from here would be as easy as escaping from the States.''

''What do you want me to do with him, sir?'' the guard asked Dimitri.

''Get him back to work,'' said Dimitri. ''If he drops, let him lie in the dirt. He's not going anywhere—are you, Hans? And remember, if you cause any more trouble, we cut your rations in half.''

The fire had faded from Karl Ross's eyes. His voice was a whimper. ''But it's such a very little bit already. Maybe if I ate a little more, I could work better. Nothing much. Some extra margarine, maybe. It makes the bread taste so much better.''

''Well, if you're very good, we'll see about that,'' said Dimitri, smiling. ''We might even give you some meat on Sundays. How does that sound, Hans? You don't mind my calling you 'Hans,' do you, Hans?''

"No, no, not at all," Karl Ross said. "Please, forget my little outburst. It was the sun. Yes, a touch of sun. A little meat, you said? Maybe this Sunday? It has been so long."

Karl Ross picked up his hoe and began hacking at the weeds with as much vigor as his bent body could muster. Dimitri watched with a smirk on his face, then climbed back into the jeep. Frank and Joe, both feeling queasy, followed him, and the jeep drove off.

"Guess you've seen enough," Dimitri said. "You get the idea how we operate here."

"Yeah, we've got the idea," said Frank, masking his disgust.

"Sure do," agreed Joe.

"Anyway, you won't be working out here," said Dimitri. "You've been assigned to the ranch house staff. Easy duty. You even have your living quarters there, so you don't have to live in the barracks. I'll take you there now to be briefed."

When they reached the ranch house—a rambling, two-story, colonial-style structure built around a central courtyard—Dimitri offered a few words of caution. "Like I said, it's easy duty, but there is one hitch. You're going to be working right under the chief, and sometimes he's—well, a little extreme. The guys before you made the mistake of acting surprised at some of the stuff he did—and they're out guarding the jungle now, fighting mosquitoes. So, if you know what's good for you, you'll keep your noses clean and do exactly what you're told."

Dimitri left Frank and Joe with the front door guard, who said to them, "You can pick up your gear and bedding and get settled later. The chief wants you right now. On the double."

"Where do we go?" asked Frank.

"Down that hall there and through the door at the end," said the guard. "It leads to the courtyard."

"What do you think?" asked Joe as he and Frank started down the wide, high-ceilinged hall. "Is it worth fifty thousand a month?"

"It's not bad," Frank said as the two brothers looked around at the sweeping Spanish-tiled stairways, huge oil paintings, and antique carpets. "But even that much money isn't enough to keep an organization like this going. Think about it. The house in Florida, the yacht, the private railroad, the ranch—it's got to cost more than a small country."

"The world's greatest scam for the world's biggest crooks." Joe shook his head in disbelief. "Can you imagine how Karl Ross reacted when he got here and found out what he'd laid out his money for? A prison a lot worse than the one he was escaping. Not such a Perfect Getaway."

"At least they haven't killed him," said Frank.

"Yeah—but that's the question. Why haven't they? They've gotten all they can from him." Joe paused to straighten what looked like a small but genuine Rembrandt painting.

"Lucky we got assigned to headquarters," Frank said. "This'll make it a lot easier to fill in all the blanks about what's going on here."

"There's one blank I want filled in right away," said Joe.

"What's that?" asked Frank.

"What Dimitri said, that bit about the chief acting extreme," said Joe. "What could be more extreme than what we've already seen and heard around here?"

Suddenly, through the half-open door leading to the courtyard, there came a hideous human scream.

"You know, Joe," said Frank, "I've got a hunch we're about to find out."

Chapter

11

THE ONLY INHABITANTS of the large central courtyard were half a dozen bright green parrots cackling at one another in the branches of a twenty-foot palm tree. The entire courtyard was filled with lush, tropical trees, flowers, and plants in an apparent effort to bring some of the jungle into the heart of the ranch complex. In the center of this miniature jungle, an elaborate fountain paved with hand-painted tiles sent streams of water up into the humid air.

Frank and Joe were in no mood to enjoy the scenery, though. Another horrible scream pierced the air, and this time it was clear that the sound was coming from behind a closed door at the opposite end of the courtyard.

"Come on," said Frank, and he led the way

through the trees, causing the parrots to squawk indignantly overhead.

"Frank, maybe we should—" Joe said as they reached the far door.

"Ssh," Frank warned him and cracked the door open to peer inside. Just then another nerve-shattering scream washed over them.

"I told you, I don't have any!" a voice cried out. Frank hestiated. The voice was familiar. He motioned to Joe, and the two boys slipped through the door.

This section of the ranch was radically different from the main entryway, and something about it made the Hardys' skin crawl. The narrow, low-ceilinged hall was painted antiseptic white. The lighting was fluorescent. The floor was green linoleum.

"Looks like the infirmary at school," Joe whispered.

Voices came from a room at the end of the hall, where a door had been left ajar. The two voices were too low now to decipher, but they sounded familiar. Frank and Joe moved toward them and cautiously looked into the room.

Igor, his clothes torn and muddy and his face cut, was sitting in a dentist's chair. An IV plugged into his wrist fed what looked like a glucose solution into his bloodstream.

The other man was the chief. He wore his khakis and cowboy hat and was standing on the other side of the chair. Near him was a table loaded down with a lie detector, a voice-stress analyzer, and other complicated electronic equipment that even Frank had never seen before. The chief held a syringe in one hand and was adjusting his equipment with the other, while talking to Igor in a low monotone. When he saw Frank and Joe, he stopped talking.

Remembering Dimitri's warning, Frank and Joe were careful to show no surprise at the scene. Keeping their faces expressionless, they entered the room, saluted, and said in unison, "Reporting for duty as ordered, sir."

"Glad you're on board, boys," the chief said, his western accent more pronounced than ever. "I was just warming up Igor here a little bit. Seems he's a bit shy about telling me where he's stashed his cache."

"I told you, I have no cache," Igor protested, unable to take his eyes off the syringe, whose tip bubbled with an odd-looking blue liquid. "Please, you have to believe me."

"Sure I believe you, partner," said the chief, smiling. "Just like I believe all the folks who come visiting us here. All those poor, poor fellows. None of them with a red cent stashed away, except for what they brought with them. And you, you don't even have that anymore, do you?"

The chief checked the level of the IV solution. Then he held up the syringe and squeezed it until a tiny blue bubble dripped down the side. "Yep, poor old Igor here had the unfortunate idea of trying to cut out once he saw it wasn't quite the palace he'd envisioned," the chief said, reaching for Igor's free arm. "Seems he jumped the train as it was slowing down outside the ranch. The guards caught him, naturally. And if they hadn't, the snakes sure would have. The penalty for an escape attempt at Rancho Getaway is the forfeiting of all a man's available money. Sad to say, Mr. Igor here doesn't seem to have the extra savings for even one more night alive."

"I liquidated all my assets before I left the States," Igor babbled frantically, watching in horror as the chief prepared to inject him with the poisonous-looking blue chemical. "Gave it all away. I didn't think I'd need it anymore—"

"That plus a dollar will get you a cup of coffee," the chief said impatiently. "Now, this won't hurt much. You'll just feel a cold shiver up your spine. Kind of like a rattlesnake bite. Hold him down, boys, will you? He's squirming around too much."

Frank and Joe stepped forward hesitantly and placed their hands on Igor's shoulders, ignoring the desperate, mute appeal for help in his eyes. The chief brought the syringe closer to the surface of Igor's skin and lined up the needle with a vein. Joe's eyes sought out Frank's in alarm. Each knew what the other was thinking. How long could they let this go on? Igor might be a crook, but nobody deserved this.

The chief pulled back his finger to plunge the

needle in. Joe tensed his legs, ready to tackle him in an instant.

"Okay, okay, you win!" Igor's voice was hoarse with fear. "I've got savings. Swiss bank accounts. You can have it all. Just get that thing away from me!"

The chief smiled and stepped back. Relieved, Frank and Joe released their hold on Igor. "I knew you'd come to your senses," the chief said, setting the syringe on the table and reaching for a pad and pencil. "If you'll just give me the account numbers, I think we might have ourselves a deal."

As Igor, half-mad with relief and fear, rattled off a string of account numbers from memory, Joe and Frank exchanged glances. "Extreme" wasn't the word for the chief. "Crazy" was closer.

Except that if the chief was crazy, it was like a fox.

A rabidly cruel fox.

"That's all?" the chief mumbled as he copied down the last of the account numbers. There were almost a dozen, all in Swiss and offshore banks, the kind that operate by number only instead of by name, appearance, or proper ID. "You wouldn't be holding out on me again, I hope, Igor."

"Are you kidding? Money's not everything, you know."

The chief chuckled. "Untie him," he commanded the Hardys as he started out of the room. "We'll go inside and get these funds transferred so Igor here can relax and take a shower in his room. You two come along, to keep guard."

The chief's office was ultramodern, except for pictures of the Old West and the mounted head of a longhorn steer that jutted out of the wall behind his chrome-and-marble desk.

The chief motioned for Igor to sit down facing the desk and ordered Frank and Joe to stand guard near the door. "Make yourself comfortable," he said to Igor. "I'm going to check these little old numbers out. We've got a communications setup here that can do that in no time flat." He started to leave, then paused. "I forgot," he said to the Hardys. "You two haven't been issued weapons yet. Until that happens, you can use this."

The chief took a pearl-handled six-gun out of a cabinet near the desk and tossed it to Joe. Then he left the room.

As soon as he was gone, shutting the door behind him, Igor turned eagerly to the Hardys.

"You two have to help me escape," he said. "That money I promised you before—well, I'll triple it. Quadruple it. Anything."

"What are you going to pay us with?" said Frank, keeping up a show of suspicion. No sense in blowing his and Joe's cover.

"Yeah," Joe seconded him. "Looks like the chief has all your cash."

Despite his sorry state, Igor looked at him with contempt. "You think I gave him all my bank account numbers? Don't be a fool. With crooks like him, you've always got to keep your highest cards back, just in case he threatens you again. Those accounts I gave him were chicken feed. I've got something worth more than all of them put together. Millions, I tell you, millions."

"Millions?" Frank said, pretending to think it over. "What could be worth that much?"

"Information, my friend." Igor leaned toward him, and the Hardys again saw the look of raw desperation they'd witnessed when the chief had threatened to put him out. He was a cornered animal, they realized, and he'd fight tooth and claw before allowing himself to become someone else's prey. "Stock tips. Insider scams. Who's going to make the next takeover bid and when. I put half the people in the top five hundred where they are today. I can even do a little blackmail if I have to. Why do you think I'm on the run? Because I've got a direct line to the really big money, boys, and I know how to redirect it."

While Igor was trying to persuade the boys to help him, Frank was thinking fast. He and Joe had to get out of this place, anyway, had to report this ranch to the authorities. There were valid reasons for taking Igor along. They could hand him over to the law, which would make him pay for his crimes. Whatever those crimes were, they couldn't be bad enough to justify leaving him to the chief.

"Sounds good," he said cautiously to Igor. "But I have to see what my buddy here thinks."

"It's a deal," said Joe. "But remember, we don't let you out of our sight until we have the money in our hands. And I'll have *this* in my hand all the time." He indicated the six-gun he was holding.

"Afraid that gun's not much good to you," said the chief's voice. They whirled around to see him standing in the doorway. In his hand was another six-gun, the twin of the one he'd given Joe. "That gun I tossed you isn't loaded. But the one I have is."

Frank realized instantly what had happened. "You've got your office bugged!"

"Smart boy," said the chief, and made a brief gesture with his gun toward the mounted steer head on the wall. "That steer has ears. But you should have been smarter sooner. You two boys made the same mistake as the two boys you're replacing. They stood here in this very room with that big-deal financier from New York, Karl Ross was his name, and they listened to him when he talked about the money he was holding out on me. You won't be seeing them around anymore. And as for Ross, he's not going to be bribing anybody else, because he's got no money and no special contacts left to bribe them with."

"A setup," Igor murmured, unable to believe

he'd been had. "You were planning this all along."

"Sure I was, partner." The chief swung his icy gaze to the exhausted man. "Even your liquid assets aren't enough to make a profit on a place like this. What I need is power. Knowledge. Leverage. I need to own people. That's what gives the ranch the sweet smell of success."

Slumped in his chair, Igor looked like a deflated balloon. The presence of lie detectors and similar equipment in the back room clearly made more sense to him now. With a gesture of defeat, he picked up a pen and starting writing down names on a piece of paper.

"That's right," the chief said, peering over his shoulder. "Whatever you can give me. Just make sure I can make it stick. You already told me what I can get out of this—'millions, I tell you, millions.' "

Igor didn't answer. He continued writing, lost in silent despair.

"Now that our business is over with, I get to deal with you two boys," said the chief, smiling. "That's the fun part. I figure we can have a little lassoing contest in the corral out back. I used to be a pretty fair cowhand years ago. I grew up on a ranch like this, but smaller. I'll tell you what. If you can make it to the corral gate, you'll get to work in the fields. If you don't make it, you're going to fertilize them. I'm afraid the two boys before you were a mite slow—disappointing, really. I'd hoped for more of a challenge. But you two look very fit. Maybe you'll give me a run for your money. Or I guess I should say, a run for your lives."

The chief looked Frank and Joe up and down as though he were inspecting livestock. "I'll take you one by one. Who wants to be first?"

"Me," Frank and Joe said at the same time.

"Believe me, my buddy is as slow as molasses," Joe added quickly, before Frank could say anything. "He's strictly long distance, not a sprinter like me."

The chief said nothing, just continued to size them up. Then he nodded. "Okay, I believe you. You first, boy. And remember, I want to see some speed."

"You'll get it," said Joe with a show of bravado. "No way you're going to get that rope around me, old man."

The chief grinned, looking delighted. "That's what I like to see, a little spunk. Roping you in is going to be the most fun I've had in a month of Sundays." He turned to the others. "You two can wait here while I play my little game with your friend."

Holding his gun on Joe, he motioned him out of the office, then locked the door as he left. He and Joe walked back to the large corral behind the ranch house, an elaborate construction with high walls of corrugated metal, an attached stable, and all the paraphernalia necessary for a real big-time rodeo.

"Go on, get in there," the chief said, pushing Joe into the corral and locking the gate after him. "I don't figure you're going to make it to the gate," he explained. "But even if you do, if my horse stumbles or something, you're still not going to get away. The only thing you're going to escape is the cemetery."

"Fair enough," said Joe, doing some stretch exercises to loosen up his muscles. "Just watch my dust."

The chief shook his head. "It will be fun cutting you down to size. Maybe I'll even put my brand on you." There was a nasty edge to his voice. "I wonder where I should put it. The center of your forehead might look good. Move on out to the middle, now. I'll be there in a minute."

Joe watched the chief head for the stable, then turned and surveyed the large corral. Halfway across it was a long distance for a sprint. Joe started across, slowly. From the stable, he heard the whinny of a horse. Then suddenly, behind him, he heard the crack of a gun.

The chief sat astride a palomino in a cubicle near the gate. The six-gun in his right hand was pointed in the air, and his left hand rested on the lasso that was wrapped around the saddle horn. "Coming out of chute number three!" the chief shouted in a rodeo announcer's voice, and shoved the gun into the holster at his hip. The door of the cubicle shot up, and the horse raced right for Joe as the chief gave a wild, ear-shattering whoop.

At the first sound, Joe started moving, as fast a start as he had ever made. His feet were pumping beneath him, his heart was pounding in his chest, and his lungs felt as if they would burst. He rounded the corral, approaching the gate from the opposite side, steadily getting closer.

Then he felt the rope drop down over his shoulders and tighten.

And he heard the chief's cry of triumph. "You lost, boy. You're dead!"

Chapter

12

THAT WAS WHAT Joe had been waiting for.

As soon as he felt the rope tighten around him, he came to an abrupt halt. At the same moment he grabbed the rope in both hands and yanked with every ounce of his strength, praying that he had made his move fast enough to stop the chief from bracing himself in the saddle.

It worked, just as Joe had gambled it would. Caught by surprise, the chief didn't have time either to brace himself or to let go of the rope. Instead, his hands instinctively tightened on the rope, and he flew out of the saddle, hitting the ground flat on his face.

Before the chief could roll over and draw his gun, Joe straddled him and grabbed the gun from his holster.

Joe stood up, shrugging off the rope that still

hung loosely around him. "Okay, Chief, on your feet. The game's over, and guess who won? In case you don't know, keep your hands in the air—or as you'd say, reach for the sky, partner."

The chief looked at the gun, and followed orders. But his eyes were blazing. "You're not going to get away with this, boy," he snarled. "You're going to pay."

"Unless you follow orders, *you're* going to get paid off—with this," said Joe and raised the gun so that it was pointing right between the chief's eyes. He wanted to make sure the chief believed he would use it—because Joe had a feeling that he wouldn't be able to, even in a pinch.

"Okay, okay, boy," the chief said hurriedly. "Just be careful of that piece. The trigger's kind of sensitive. The least little thing will set it off."

"Fine," said Joe. "Make sure you don't supply that least little thing."

The chief didn't have to be told where they were going. He unlocked the gate and headed out of the dusty corral and back to his office, where he unlocked the door without being told.

Igor's mouth dropped open when he saw the chief enter, with Joe following, gun in hand. "How did you—" he started to ask.

But before he could finish, Frank grinned and said, "I figured you'd pull it off."

"You should have seen it," Joe said.

"Both you boys better fasten onto one idea now," said the chief, careful not to make any sudden moves but not hiding the menace in his voice. "No way you're getting away with this. You can't escape. There's jungle all around. And the longer you hold me, the rougher I'm going to be on you when you realize you can't escape and have to give up."

"Maybe he's right," Igor said. "Perhaps we can make a deal."

"You never learn, do you?" said Joe with disgust. "You can't make a deal with someone like him."

"Besides, we won't have to make a deal—not when we can make tracks," said Frank, his eyes lighting up.

Joe recognized that light. Frank had an idea.

"What kind of tracks?" asked Igor.

"Railroad tracks," said Frank. "We arrived by train, and we can leave the same way."

By now Joe had the idea. He pointed at the chief with his gun. "Yeah, we've got our ticket right here."

"What makes you boys think—" the chief began.

"We don't think, we *know*," said Frank. "We *know* that you're going to pick up that phone and order the train to get ready. We *know* that you're going to order that all your 'guests' be rounded up and put in a ventilated boxcar. We *know* that the train's going to pull out of here in a couple of hours, with us and you aboard. And, oh yes, we *know* that there'll be enough provisions on it to feed everybody until that yacht arrives on its regular run to the coast and you can give orders for it to take us back to the States."

"You want to know *how* we know all that?" Joe chimed in. *"We* know that *you* know what'll happen to you if you don't do just what we say."

The chief looked at the gun staring him in the face, and picked up the phone.

He made three calls, never taking his eyes from the gun. With the first call he ordered that the train be readied; with the second, that the boxcars be loaded with all the guests from the ranch; and with the third, that four days' worth of food and drink be loaded in another boxcar.

When he was asked if any men would be required to go along as guards, the chief gave a glance at the gun and said, no, the two men he had with him would be enough.

That was the only question he was asked. Frank, listening closely for any signs of trickery, wasn't surprised. The chief was the kind of boss who gave orders and demanded unquestioning obedience.

Meanwhile, Igor was rejoicing. "Great work," he said. "When we get out of this, I'll give you that bonus I promised. Or, if you prefer, you can give me that money to invest, and I'll make you really rich."

"Thanks, we might consider that," said Frank, barely able to suppress a grin. Igor simply couldn't pass up an opportunity to try a scam, even under these circumstances.

"Yeah," said Joe, keeping a straight face, too. "We could use the help of a financial whiz like you."

Igor gave them a genial smile. Then his expression clouded. "There's one thing I don't understand. Why are we taking along those others? They all must be broke by now. What good are they?"

Frank tried to think of an explanation that would satisfy Igor. "They might have money still hidden away. You never know."

"I doubt it—but I'll leave that to you," said Igor. "I believe in the free enterprise system." He rubbed his hands together in anticipation.

Frank and Joe knew that this wasn't the time to let Igor know that he and the others were heading back to the States to be put into the hands of the law. Frank did figure, though, that it was time to find out more about Igor.

"Say, Igor," he said, "since we're going to be partners, we should know your real name."

"I understand. It never hurts to be prudent," said Igor, still smiling his oily smile. "Perhaps you've read about me. My name is Tanner. Adolf Tanner."

Frank and Joe glanced at each other. Adolf Tanner, Gregory Miller's boss. The guy who had disappeared, leaving Marcie's father holding the bag.

"Adolf Tanner," said Frank, wrinkling his brow, pretending to try to remember the name. "Seems to me I did read something about you. You vanished, but somebody working with you got caught."

"Some guy called Muller or Milner or something like that," added Joe.

"Miller," Tanner said. "Gregory Miller. He worked under me, not with me. Your typical Boy Scout. Before I left, I doctored my books to make it look like he was the one milking my company. For insurance, I had one of my men stick a briefcase full of cash in his closet to make it look like he was planning to escape. If I'm lucky, the police will also suspect him of doing away with me to cover his thefts. He'll wind up in jail, and I'll be in the clear. Beautiful, you have to admit."

"I have to hand it to you, you are one shrewd operator," said Frank.

Now, especially, both Hardys couldn't wait to get back to the States. They had solved the mystery they had set out to solve. They had found out the truth about Marcie's father. They had caught the real crook, and it should be simple enough to prove that Mr. Miller had only called Perfect Getaway in an effort to track down Tanner. How he had heard about it, they'd have to ask him later. Now all they had to do was deliver their catch.

They didn't have long to wait for the delivery mechanism to start operating.

In half an hour the chief's phone began ringing.

Each time it rang, the chief picked up the receiver and merely listened to the caller. Then he said, "Very good," hung up, and relayed the information.

The train was made ready and turned around to head back toward the sea.

The supplies were loaded into a boxcar.

Finally, the prisoners were loaded aboard.

"Time to move out," said Joe. "I'm putting this gun in my pocket, but my hand's going to be resting on it. One wrong move from you, Chief, and you'll find out how fast I can pull the trigger. Hope I'm coming through loud and clear."

The chief nodded. With Joe right behind him, he led the way out of the room. He looked neither to his right nor his left as the group passed the guards at the entrance of the ranch house and climbed into a waiting jeep, Joe sitting close beside the chief. The sun had set, and a full moon was just rising, bathing the land in a silvery glow.

The jeep drove them to the ghostly train, shimmering in the moonlight. Only a dim light from the train's interior added to that illumination. Security, as always, was tight.

Dimitri was waiting with a squad of men. He opened the jeep door and stood at attention as the chief climbed out, followed by the others, with Joe in the lead.

"Hey, where do you think you're going, Igor?"

Dimitri barked. "You go back in the boxcar with the other prisoners."

Tanner opened his mouth to protest, then caught himself. It was clearly all he could do to keep from winking at Joe and Frank as he responded meekly, "Yes, sir. Sorry, sir."

After he was led off, the chief and the Hardys entered the passenger car, followed by Dimitri.

"Will there be anything else, Chief?" Dimitri asked.

The chief's eyes flicked around to meet Joe's hard gaze. Then he looked at Dimitri and said, "No. You're dismissed. Tell the engineer to get the train moving."

After Dimitri left, the chief and the Hardys sat silently in their compartment until the train started rolling.

"Glad to see you're being sensible," Joe said. "That means you're going to stay alive. Don't look so mad, though. Life in jail won't be so bad. I'm sure you'll be out in twenty or thirty years."

"You—" began the chief. But when Joe pulled out his gun, the chief swallowed the rest of his sentence.

"Time to make some changes," said Frank, checking out the window to make sure that the ranch was out of sight. "Let's pay a visit to the engineer."

Herding the chief ahead of them, they moved forward through the passenger car and then through a door that connected it with the engineer's compartment.

The engineer had the train controls set on automatic. He was sitting back in his seat with his eyes closed.

Frank tapped him on the shoulder. He looked up, saw the chief, and leapt to his feet.

"Sorry, sir," he babbled. "Just taking a little break. Won't happen again, I—"

Then he saw the gun in Joe's hand.

"We want you to do us a favor," Joe said. "Show us how to run this thing. We want to expand our occupational skills."

A half hour later the chief and the engineer were tied up in the passenger car, and Joe and Frank were at the controls.

"Tanner seemed a little disappointed that he had to go second-class."

"I'm afraid Tanner has a lot of disappointments coming up," said Joe as he moved a lever to speed up the train. "This is fun. When I was a kid, I always wanted to drive a train."

"Okay, Casey Jones, just keep your eyes on the tracks and don't lose your head," said Frank.

"You know me," said Joe, increasing the speed still more.

"That's the trouble," said Frank. "I don't want to have survived all of this only to wind up in an old-fashioned train wreck."

"No problem," said Joe. "Clear track ahead."

Frank couldn't argue. The front lights of

the train had come on when the train entered the tunnel formed by the foliage overhead. The gleaming rails stretched unbroken into the darkness.

After a while Joe rubbed his eyes. "I have to admit, this job is tougher than it looks. Those rails are almost hypnotic, and we haven't had a decent night of sleep since we left Bayport."

"You're right about that," said Frank. "Good thing we're practically at the end of the tunnel." He couldn't stop his mouth from opening in a wide yawn.

Then his eyes widened, and his yawn froze. For a second all he could do was make a gasping sound.

Then he choked out, "Put on the brakes—or we'll crash!"

He didn't really have to say anything. Joe, too, had spotted the felled trees lying across the track. He yanked on the brakes and started breathing again only when he felt the train come to a stop with a loud hiss and an ear-piercing screech.

"Let's get out and see—" Frank began.

But he and Joe only had to glance out the window behind them to see what had happened.

Dimitri was standing there, gun in hand.

And from the darkness behind Dimitri came a voice that they recognized all too well.

"Hello, Hardys. Long time, no see."

Chapter
13

FRANK AND JOE instantly recognized the squat man with a mustache who held them at gunpoint.

"Alex!" Frank managed to say.

"How did you get here?" said Joe in a stunned voice, remembering their last sight of Alex in the mansion on the Florida key.

Alex smiled. "Me, explain anything to brilliant detectives like the Hardys?" he said sarcastically. "I wouldn't be so presumptuous. I'll let you try to figure it out, until we get you back to the ranch. If you still don't know, the chief can explain—before he tells you what he's decided to do with you." Alex's smile widened. "I want to be around for *that*. Should be fun."

A half hour later Frank and Joe were back at the ranch, along with the chief, Alex, and a squad of armed guards. They had all been flown there in the same helicopter that Alex and the guards had used to beat the train to the end of the tracks. A few men had been left behind to turn the train around and return its human cargo to captivity.

When they were all in the chief's office, Alex asked the two boys, "Well, have you figured out how I got here yet?"

Frank had been thinking about it the whole trip back. "You must have had some kind of emergency plan, in case somebody got through your security shield," he said. "I should have thought of that. The chief would want to cover his bases in case somebody goofed up."

"Now you're talking horse sense, boy," said the chief. "Too bad you thought about it too late. As soon as that fool you put to sleep on the ship woke up, he found those two recruits tied up and reported what had happened to the captain. The captain then went to his safe and got out a sealed envelope he'd been told was to be used only if somebody slipped past what you call our 'security shield.' There was a phone number in there. As soon as the ship got to the nearest island, he made the call and talked to Alex, who took it from there. The captain never even had to break radio silence."

"All according to the chief's faultless plan," said Alex, shamelessly flattering the old man. "The chief thought of everything. All I had to do was open my own sealed envelope, which gave me a flight plan to the ranch. I flew down in a company plane, and when I arrived here and heard that a couple of new recruits named Mike and Dave were with the chief and the prisoners on a train trip to the coast, it was easy to see what was happening. All I had to do was load up the ranch helicopter with men and cut you off.'' He slapped his thigh with boisterous amusement. ''Sure did get a kick out of seeing the look on your faces. You looked like you'd seen a ghost.''

''And now we'll see what's going to happen to you,'' said the chief, enjoying the look that now appeared on the Hardys' faces. ''We could just kill you. A couple of bullets in the back of the neck and that would be that. But after what you've done to me, that's not enough. I think you need to sweat a little.''

The old man pulled off his cowboy hat as he walked close to the two boys. His voice hardened as he wiped the sweat from his face and said, ''Fact is, boys, I want to see the two of you sweat blood. And I know how to make you do it.''

As he watched the brothers' faces tighten in apprehension, his booming laugh filled the room. ''I don't think I'll tell you how. I'll let you start sweating now, and you can sweat the whole night through. Then tomorrow I'll let you in on my little surprise. We'll see if you boys can really take it.''

He turned to his guards. ''Put them in the lockup. And turn up the heat.''

* * *

The lockup was a windowless white room. There was no furniture—not even a crude cot or bolted-down chair such as one would expect to find in the lowliest jail cell. Hanging down above the door was a 500-watt light that could have driven away the shadows on a city block. In that small room, the glare reflected off the stone floor and the steel door and turned the tiny chamber into an oven.

Joe used the palm of his hand to wipe away the sweat pouring down his face. "Whew! Must be a hundred degrees in here."

Frank was sweating just as hard. "Right, and they didn't leave us a drop of water."

"Then that means we've got to get out of here—fast. But how?" asked Joe.

Frank started to say something but then, grinning ruefully, put a finger to his lips to indicate that they'd have to work in silence. They couldn't afford to let the chief overhear their plans. Then he realized that he had no plan. Shrugging his shoulders, he sat down on the floor to think. And sweat.

Joe wouldn't join him. He couldn't. His restless nature demanded that he do *something*. He paced around and around the cell. Finally he dropped to the floor beside Frank and said in a whisper, "I hope you've figured a way out of this box. I've looked over the doors, the walls, the floor—every inch of it—and I think they've really got us this time."

Frank replied in a voice no louder than his brother's, "Sometimes all we can do is wait and save our energy for when there's an opening."

"Listen, Frank," snapped Joe, "waiting I can put up with, but baking's too much. I'm going to knock out this light, at least. Much more of this heat, and come morning all they're going to find are a couple of crispy critters."

Joe backed up against the far wall and charged full speed at the door. The instant before he would have crashed into the weighty steel sheet, he leapt skyward like a basketball player going up for a slam dunk. At the top of his jump he caught hold of the heavy steel pipe from which the light was suspended. Slowly, feeling the heat of the scalding globe only inches away, he pulled himself up until he could brace one arm over the bar.

As he reached out to smash the bulb Frank suddenly jumped to his feet. "Wait," he said sharply.

Joe stared disbelievingly at his brother.

"Frank, if you have an idea, it better be a fast one. I don't know which I'm going to do first— fry or fall down."

"Then be quiet and listen," Frank said softly. "Don't unscrew the bulb, unscrew the *fixture*. There should be some slack in the wire. If we can pull it down as far as the door, then maybe we can give the guards a hot welcome."

"All right," whispered Joe enthusiastically.

"Then we can arrange for one of those openings you were talking about."

With no tools and only their thin khaki shirts to protect them from the searing heat of the light, it took Frank and Joe hours to set their trap. By the time they were finished, they figured it was only a couple of hours before dawn.

"Now, how do we issue invitations to this party?" asked Joe.

"Easy," Frank answered. He wrapped his hands in the scorched remains of his khaki shirt and, grasping the now-dangling wire close to the bulb, he smashed the globe against the door and began screaming.

After the hours of silence, Frank's cries tore open the night. The two boys could hear the sound of running footsteps.

"What's going on in there?" a gruff voice demanded.

"The light exploded and I think my brother's all cut up!" Joe said urgently.

"He's going to be worse than that if he doesn't shut up," the man growled. Frank's screams continued.

"Your boss won't like it if Frank's hurt when he comes for him," Joe said pleadingly.

"Okay, but both of you stand back while I open up the door," the guard grumbled.

The boys listened to the sound of a key turning in the lock. The minute it clicked open, Frank, still holding the wire, jabbed the metal base of the shattered bulb against the steel door. The darkness was illuminated by a blue flash! And the boys heard a single, choked cry as the surge of electricity flowed through the steel door and into the man behind it.

Frank jerked the bulb back, and Joe reached for the door handle. When the door swung open, the cool night air tasted like springwater to the two parched prisoners.

After carrying the unconscious guard into the cell, they bound and gagged him with the remains of their shirts. Locking the door behind them, they took his keys and set out to explore the house.

"The first thing we have to do is find some weapons," Joe whispered. "I won't go back in that room. And I don't want to know what else the chief has planned for us."

"Me, neither, but if we want to get out of here alive, we have to get some help," Frank replied as he opened the outer door and inched carefully into the courtyard. The sky was the hazy gray of the last hours before dawn.

Across the courtyard, the boys could see the ranch-house guard, tipped back in one of the easy chairs sleeping.

"I'd hate to be in his shoes when the chief finds us gone," murmured Joe.

"Be quiet or we won't be." Frank eased open the door to the main hall of the house.

Once they were inside, Joe indicated that they

should go upstairs, but Frank shook his head. He pointed up and mouthed the word "guests." Then he pointed at the heavy oak door at the end of the hall and pantomimed the words "the chief." An angry look appeared on Joe's face and he began striding toward the door.

Frank grabbed him by the arm and whispered fiercely, "We don't want him now, Joe. What we want is a way out of here. He has to have some way of communicating with the outside world. If we can get a message out, we can hide in the jungle and wait until the cavalry arrives."

Joe kept going, almost dragging Frank down the hall. Just before they reached the chief's door, they came to a much less impressive oak door bearing a sign that read: RESTRICTED— STAFF ONLY. It was locked, but the keys they had taken from the unconscious guard let them in.

There, in a tiny alcove, they found themselves facing three doors, each bearing a lettered sign. When they read them—LOUNGE, ARMORY, COMMUNICATIONS—Frank punched the air and whispered a heartfelt, "All ri-i-ight!"

Joe turned to him and said in a barely audible voice, "I think Santa has just delivered, even if he did forget the swimsuit."

A moment's celebration was all they could afford. As soon as Joe had the armory door open, he tossed the keys to Frank, who entered the communications room.

The armory was a policeman's nightmare—a

terrorist's dream come true. Joe was surrounded by racks of M-16s. Crates of .223 caliber, full-metal-jacketed ammunition lined the wall. And in a cabinet at the back of the storeroom were enough C-4 plastic explosives to move the ranch house and all its occupants into another country. Joe realized that for the first time in many hours he was smiling. He cleared a space on the table in the center of the room and went to work.

When Frank walked into the communications room, it was like coming home. Low counters lined the walls, and sitting on them were two computers and an extremely sophisticated radio setup.

When Frank booted up the two computers, he immediately discovered two things. First, one of the computers was used to do nothing except direct a rooftop microwave antenna that linked the ranch to the nearest phone system. Second, the other computer—the one used to assemble a message to go out over the antenna—required a password. A password he didn't have. He settled in before the computer, determined to use every hacker trick he knew.

When Joe walked in about forty minutes later, he stared over his brother's shoulder at the CRT. He watched as the words PLEASE ENTER PASS-WORD appeared on the screen, followed by the key clicks of Frank trying one stunt after another.

"Why do you always try the hard way, Frank?" Joe asked. "Let me go get the chief.

He'll tell us his password if I ask him just right."
Frank knew how his brother would ask—with his
fists.

"Give me a few more minutes. So far I've
figured out that the password is six characters
long and that the only person who uses this
computer is the chief himself." Frank didn't look
up from the keyboard as he spoke.

"Well, don't let me rush you," Joe said calmly,
"but I've planted a few surprises around the
house that are due to go off in about—let's see—
eight minutes."

Frank's fingers froze as he turned to gaze at his
grinning brother.

The look on Joe's face told Frank all he needed
to know. As he turned back toward the computer,
he said, "And I guess we don't want to be anywhere nearby when your 'surprises' go off, do
we?"

"Nope."

Frank mentally reviewed the list of words he'd
tried, the ways he'd attempted to bypass the
computer's security system. For once, he was
sure that the chief had been too confident. He felt
as if the answer to this puzzle was right on the tip
of his tongue. Yes!—he had it.

"Hey, Joe, if you wanted one word to describe
the chief, what would it be?" he asked. He answered the question himself as he typed in the six
letters needed to control the computer, C-O-W-
B-O-Y. The screen went blank for a moment, and

then a menu of all the computer's functions and files appeared.

Frank was totally in his element now. As Joe counted off the seconds, he scanned a file here, set up a short program there, and set up a message that would end up on his hacker friend Phil Cohen's computer back in Bayport.

"Frank, if we don't go *right* now, we are going to get caught when the fireworks go off," Joe said, his voice tight with tension.

"Just one more thing," Frank replied. "I want to see this file called 'auction.' I think that it has the answer to a lot of our qu—"

"Look, answers won't matter in just about one minute." Joe grabbed his brother's arm and literally dragged him out of the room and into the hallway. Speed, not silence, was what was important now. The sound of their footsteps must have awakened the guard, because as they tore through the courtyard they could hear him shouting behind them.

Joe led Frank through the gate at the back of the courtyard and toward the corral. Standing there was the chief's palomino, saddled and waiting. "Sorry about this, but I could only find one horse," Joe panted.

Two shots whistled past as Joe leapt into the saddle and Frank mounted behind him, taking a firm grip on Joe's shoulders.

"Let's go," Joe shouted, and kicked the palomino's sides. The horse got the message. It was off like a shot, racing across the grassland toward the jungle. "We'll follow the tracks," Joe shouted.

There was more gunfire coming from behind them. Just then, Frank heard a tremendous explosion. Looking back, he saw the trucks burst into flames and watched the locomotive rise up off the tracks and fall over in almost slow motion. The chief's men were all scrambling for cover.

"It'll take them a while to come after us," Joe shouted.

"It'll take them a while to figure out they're all in one piece," Frank answered. The two brothers began laughing, relieved to be, at least for the moment, safe and free.

About half a mile down the track the horse began to slow down. Joe pulled on the reins and brought it to a halt. He knew that a good horse could burst its heart running, and that was the last thing he wanted to happen to this animal. The two boys climbed off it. Joe looked at the horse's heaving flanks and the froth coming from its mouth. "Sorry to have worked you so hard, pal," Joe said. "But it was for a good cause. You can take off now." He gave it an affectionate pat on the flanks and grinned as the horse trotted easily away down the track, relieved of its double burden.

"Time to get off these tracks," said Frank. He looked at the mass of jungle on both sides of them.

"Hey, you didn't really believe that stuff they told us about this jungle being filled with alligators and snakes and jaguars, did you?" Joe said.

"Not a bit," said Frank. "Scare talk."

They pushed their way into the foliage, but it was hard going. The ground was soft, the trees thick, and vines lay like trip wire all around. A hundred different kinds of insects buzzed around their heads, all of them having a feast on every inch of exposed flesh.

"We're not leaving much of a trail," said Joe, looking behind them. "It's as if the jungle grows right back as soon as we've passed through it."

"As if it were swallowing us," said Frank. "As soon as we reach civilization, we can get hold of the police or the army or whatever they have down here, and tell them what's going on at the ranch," said Frank. "We can also contact the U.S. embassy. That'll cook the chief's goose, if it wasn't cooked already."

"Nah. I set the charges in the house small enough to just make noise. The others blew up the trucks and train," said Joe, pausing to wipe sweat off his face and brush away a cloud of gnats. "I can hardly wait until—" He suddenly gave Frank a violent shove, sending his brother sprawling.

"Hey, what the—" Frank demanded, then followed where Joe's finger was pointing.

The black snake lay where Frank had been about to step. It raised its head and looked at them with glittering, unblinking eyes. Then it hissed softly and slithered away.

"Thanks," said Frank. "I owe you one."

"Anytime," said Joe. "Here, let me help you up."

He bent over to help Frank out of the tangle of foliage in which he lay.

Before Joe could straighten up, Frank grabbed his arm and pulled him down to land face forward in the same foliage.

Joe rolled over on his back, lifted his head, and saw what had caused his brother to react with lightning speed.

The body of a jaguar, leaping from a tree branch.

The jaguar now stood motionless a few feet away, its balance restored instantly after its miss. Its eyes flicked from Joe to Frank and back again, picking its prey.

Then it let out a vicious snarl. Frank and Joe saw its haunches tensing, ready to spring. It bared its fangs and extended its claws for the kill.

Chapter

14

DESPERATELY FRANK AND JOE tried to scramble to their feet, even though they knew they didn't stand a chance of escaping so fast an animal.

The jaguar snarled again—but this time its snarl was obliterated by the crack of a rifle and the whine of a bullet.

The bullet missed, thudding into a tree behind the big cat. But it was enough to send the animal disappearing into the jungle in two giant bounds.

By this time the Hardys were on their feet. They looked around and saw the man who had saved them. Half concealed by a tree was a dark-skinned man wearing the loose cotton pants and shirt and wide-brimmed straw hat of a local farmer. But the gleaming semiautomatic rifle in his hands wasn't designed for raising crops.

Joe grinned and waved his hand. "Hey, thanks, pal!"

The man merely stood and stared at them, his face and dark eyes expressionless.

Frank looked at his brother. "You expect him to understand you? Let me try my Spanish on him."

"*What* Spanish?" asked Joe.

"Listen and find out," said Frank. He turned toward the man. "*Muchas gracias, amigo,*" he said, almost using up his entire command of the language.

The man continued to stand and stare at them. Suspicion shone in his eyes.

"Maybe he thinks we're bandits or something," Frank said to Joe. "I'll straighten him out." He turned to the man, pointed at Joe and then at himself, and said, "*Americanos.*"

Instantly the man's gun was up, pointed straight at Frank's chest.

"Uh, Frank, I think you said the wrong thing," Joe muttered.

The man indicated that they should raise their hands in the air, which they did.

Then he took a length of cord from his pocket, and gestured to indicate that Frank and Joe should lie face down on the ground, with their hands behind them, to be tied up.

Again Frank and Joe instantly obeyed.

It was Frank whose hands the man started to tie first. Which meant that it was Frank who had the chance to kick back with his feet, knocking the man off balance, and sending his rifle flying.

Instantly Joe was on his feet, finishing the job with a right to the man's jaw.

Frank stood up and looked down at the unconscious man. "That was almost too easy," he said.

"Guess the guy wasn't used to people fighting back when he had them under the gun," said Joe, kneeling down to tie the man up with his own cord.

"Well, not too many people have had the practice we've had," said Frank. He stooped down and drew the man's machete from his belt. "We can use this to hack through the jungle."

Joe retrieved the rifle. "I don't think even Dad would object to us taking this, too. This is one spot where a gun will come in handy."

"Right," said Frank. "Jaguars aren't an endangered species around here. We are."

They tied the man up and propped him against a tree. Then they revived him.

"He should be able to work himself free in an hour or two," said Frank as he started to slash a trail through the undergrowth with the machete. Then he said, "Hey, what do we have here?"

"Some kind of path," said Joe. "This trip gets easier and easier. Now we can really make time."

"What say we try jogging?" said Frank. "See how a sprinter like you can do over the long run."

"Okay, marathon man," said Joe, breaking into a jog. "First one to run out of steam is a—"

A burst of semiautomatic weapon fire plowed a line of bullets right in front of Joe's feet, bringing the two of them to an abrupt halt.

Out of the undergrowth stepped four soldiers in camouflage uniforms and helmets. All carried semiautomatic rifles.

Frank and Joe didn't have to be told to drop the machete and rifle and raise their hands high.

"They probably think we're guerrillas," Frank muttered to Joe.

"Yeah, that rifle I was carrying didn't help," said Joe. "Guess Dad was right, after all. Guns do get you in hot water."

The soldiers advanced toward them, weapons at the ready. The expressions on their faces made it clear that they were not only ready but eager to shoot first and ask questions later.

"I'll give the magic word one more try," Frank said to Joe. Then he called out to the soldiers, *"Americanos."*

This time it worked. Their faces broke into smiles.

"Speak English?" Frank asked them hopefully. *"Inglés?"*

Still smiling, a soldier with three stripes on his uniform shook his head, but waved for them to follow him, while another soldier scooped up the rifle and machete.

Half an hour down the trail and then twenty minutes along another trail, they came to a jungle army outpost surrounded by barbed wire and machine-gun emplacements.

The soldiers led Frank and Joe through the front gate and into a tent where an officer with silver bars on his shoulders was sitting.

The sergeant spoke to him in Spanish, and then the officer said to the Hardys in perfect, unaccented English, "So you're Americans? What happened? How did you get here?"

Frank and Joe were happy to tell him, beginning with the man they had knocked out in the jungle.

The officer nodded. "A local bandit, though they call themselves guerrillas. We're stationed here to try to control them. I'll send a couple of men to pick him up. But you still didn't tell me what you were doing in this jungle originally. And I'm afraid you're going to have to. This isn't a place for tourists, you know."

"You may have a hard time believing our story," warned Frank. "But you will when you check it out."

By the time Frank and Joe finished telling him about the ranch and what was going on there, the officer's face was serious.

"You do believe us, don't you?" Frank said.

"Honest, we're telling the truth," added Joe.

The officer nodded. "I believe you. It's too incredible a story for you to have made up. And to think we believed that the ranch was an agricultural experiment."

Then he stood up. "Please wait here. I have to radio headquarters to find out how to move against this vipers' nest. It's too important for me to decide alone."

After he left, Joe said, "Hope the captain lets us come along when they go after the ranch. I'd really love to see the chief's face when they close him down."

"I just want to get my hands on Tanner and take him back to the States," said Frank. "I hate to think of Marcie's dad sweating it out in jail."

There was a smile on the captain's face when he returned. "Good news. They're sending a helicopter right away to take you to headquarters. Then, after you give them the details of how the ranch is set up, they'll move in on it immediately."

"Great," said Joe. "Think we can go along?"

"I'm sure it can be arranged," the captain said, "considering all the help you've been. Now, perhaps you'd like a bite to eat while you wait."

"Wouldn't mind," said Joe. "I could eat a horse."

"Or even a jaguar," seconded Frank with a grin.

"I'm afraid you'll have to settle for steaks," the captain said. "But I don't think you'll find them bad."

The captain's promise was an understatement. When Frank and Joe sat down in the mess tent, the steaks that were set before them were filet mignons, three inches thick, tender and juicy. With them came baked potatoes and salad. And, afterward, chocolate ice cream.

"Great," said Joe, spooning up the last of his dessert in a hurry, since he had just heard the sound of a helicopter descending outside.

"Sensational," said Frank. "Thanks a million, Captain."

"It's the least we could do," said a voice from behind them. "Condemned men are entitled to a hearty last meal."

They didn't have to turn their heads to recognize who had spoken.

Alex.

They turned to see Dimitri standing beside him. Both men were holding .45s.

Frank was the first to say what he and Joe realized at the same moment.

"You're in on this," he accused the captain.

The captain shrugged and leaned back in his chair, a lazy smile playing across his face. "I like to think of it as hardship pay. Jungle duty is no picnic. Earning a little extra from the chief eases the discomfort, and catching idiots like you relieves the boredom. Besides which, the ranch furnishes us with those excellent steaks that you so enjoyed."

"You'll earn an extra bonus for these two," Alex promised him. Then he said gloatingly to the Hardys, "I told you there was no place to go. We warn everyone about all the dangers of fleeing the ranch without mentioning the captain here. That way we can weed out the ones like you who refuse to abandon hope of escape."

Dimitri gestured with his gun for Frank and Joe to get to their feet. "Come on. The chopper is waiting—and so is the chief," he added with a nasty grin.

Prodding them with his gun barrel, Alex steered Frank and Joe into the helicopter. The Hardys took seats, trying not to think about what was in store.

The trip back to the ranch passed in silence except for the roar of the motor and the thump of the blades. Frank and Joe sat between Alex and Dimitri. Each of the Hardys had a gun barrel pressed against his side the whole way.

Waiting for them at the helicopter pad were ten guards with their guns drawn. The chief was taking no chances that Joe and Frank might spoil his fun again.

"You don't know how glad I am to see you boys," the chief said. His jaw was tight, his face pale with anger. He looked like a spoiled child who'd had his toys taken away.

Frank and Joe looked around at Joe's destructive handiwork. A pall of smoke still hung over the ranch from the burning trucks. The locomotive lay alongside the tracks like a toppled giant. When they looked back at the chief, he appeared even angrier than before. The chief waved the guards away and drew his pearl-handled revolver to cover Joe and Frank.

"Boys, we're going to have us a party. And you're going to be the entertainment," the old man said bitterly. He gestured back at the house. "Everybody'll be here. Because every last one of them has got to learn that nobody crosses me and lives."

As the boys watched, the guards began driving the men—all the men—from the house, from the barracks, in from the fields to the clearing beside the helipad. The prisoners formed a semicircle around the trio. Behind the prisoners stood the guards, guns up, ready for anything.

"We don't need trouble here," the chief shouted. "And these boys are trouble. Every once in a while, I think that you people need to be shown just exactly what can happen if we think that you're trouble!"

He stepped close to the two brothers, an evil glint in his eyes, and spoke softly, so softly that only they could hear him. "You two have any last words before I put a bullet through your brains?"

Frank looked at his brother and said, "Joe, it's been—" But he never got to finish that sentence. Joe finished it for him, shouting, "Fun!" And then the world seemed to explode around them.

Chapter

15

FRANK WAS ALIVE, but he didn't know why. He kept trying to walk until he realized that he was lying flat on his back, deaf and dizzy. All he could see was dust and smoke—and Joe sticking the muzzle of a pearl-handled revolver in the chief's ear.

What he could see of Joe's face was grim. As Frank got to his knees, he saw that the prisoners and their guards were as confused as he. But when he looked back at the ranch house—no, where the ranch house had *been*—he began to understand. And when Frank looked at Joe and the chief, Joe nodded happily. The chief simply stared, stunned by the blast and the loss of his little kingdom.

Joe was shouting something at Frank, but all Frank could do was shake his head from side to side and point at his ears. Finally, Joe dragged the chief closer to his brother and screamed at him from inches away. "Look behind you! There's the cavalry!"

When Frank turned around, he saw three large troop-carrying choppers coming in low over the tree line. They were close enough now that the men on the ground who couldn't hear them could feel them. There was no fight left in any of them. A couple of the men started a dash for the jungle, but when one of the choppers circled around to head them off, they slowed to a walk, then stopped to await their captors.

As soon as Frank and Joe saw the troops pouring out of the helicopters, they shouted as loudly as they could, *"Amigos, amigos!"*

Frank nudged his brother and muttered, "Get rid of that gun before one of these trigger-happy commandos decides to shoot you."

Joe dropped the gun like a hot potato, but kept the chief well away from it.

When the two boys saw who was walking alongside the strike force's commander, their jaws dropped. "Dad!" they shouted together.

"Hello, sons," a grinning Fenton Hardy said. "I thought I was going to get to rescue you this time, but it looks like I'm a little late. Your friend Phil got me up in the middle of the night with a wild story about you sending him somebody's secret files, and I've been flying ever since."

"Dad," said Frank, "I don't even know what

happened here, but I think that maybe Joe has some explaining to do.''

Joe laughed at his brother's amazement, as well as at the sight of the chief being herded into the corral with the rest of his men. He groped inside his pants pocket and pulled out what looked like a miniature walkie-talkie. "Well, when I spotted this in the chief's armory, I figured that if we ran into any real trouble during our escape, we could bluff our way out with this radio detonator.''

Joe stopped for a moment to look at his father and the brother who had been through so much with him. A wide grin spread across his face as he continued, "And I figured it would work even better if it wasn't a bluff, so I rigged a whole case of plastic explosives to go off if I pressed the button. I think that everything in the place went off instead.''

Frank peered at his brother, not yet certain whether he was serious. "Why didn't you tell me about that thing? We could have been blown to bits!''

"Frank," Joe said a little heatedly, "we were *about* to be blown to—''

"Calm down, guys. You can argue later. Right now, there's a gentleman over here who'd like to meet you and thank you." Fenton Hardy took one son under each arm and walked the two of them over to the lead helicopter. Sitting inside was a dignified gentleman in his late fifties. He introduced himself to them as General Juan Rodriguez of the Special Forces.

"Gentlemen," he began in his softly accented English, "I bring you personal greetings from my president. We have known about this place for some time, but were unable to move against it. You have cured a cancer on our land."

He stepped out of the chopper to survey the ranch. As he turned, staring intently at the charred rubble that had been the beautiful ranch house, at the toppled locomotive and the smoking ruin of the ranch's rolling stock, he muttered, "But we did expect to get to help in the treatment."

"General," Frank said inquiringly, "how did the chief get away with this for so long?"

"Frank," the general said with a sigh, "men are weak when it comes to money. I am certain that we will discover that a number of our young officers currently in the field have been corrupted."

"Sir," Joe said, thinking of the captain in the jungle with his juicy steaks, "there may not be all that many bad apples in your barrel. But we can show you one very bad one." He smiled at the thought of that man's arrest.

"But if you couldn't shut down the chief before," asked Frank, "why now?"

"Did you read any of the computer files you sent out to Phil?" Fenton asked his son. "They were dynamite—economic, social, and political dynamite for this country and a number of others. The chief had been using them for blackmail or simply selling the information he got out of these men to the highest bidder. The underworld railway was an equal-opportunity corrupter."

"Let me finish this part of the story," interjected the general. "One of the files that your father shared with me detailed not only the fact that the ranch was the major source of arms for the rebels who have been plaguing our country for years, but also that many of their raids had been planned at this very ranch. One of those raids cost the life of my wife." The general stopped for a moment to collect himself. "So I thank you as much as my country thanks you."

"It looks like all you have to worry about now," said Joe, trying to lighten the mood, "is whether you have enough jail cells for all these guys."

The general smiled. He took one more look around and then silently, seriously shook hands with each of the boys. "Now, my young friends, the least that my country and I can do to repay you is to put you on a helicopter and then onto a plane and fly you home for Christmas."

As soon as he said the word "Christmas," Frank clapped his hand to his forehead. "Ouch!" he said. "I just thought of something."

"What's that?" the general asked, concerned. It was apparent that he was worried that some essential part of the case that they were building was missing. Perhaps one of the important crooks had gotten away.

"Christmas!" said Frank. "Joe and I still haven't done any of our Christmas shopping!"

Joe was the first to grin in relief, followed by the other two.

"Son," said Fenton Hardy, "don't worry. There are still four more shopping days. And besides, this Christmas I think that we'll all be happy with the gift you've already given us—the two of you back home and alive."

Frank and Joe's next case:

Beautiful young heiress Tessa Carpenter thinks she needs protection, and the Hardy brothers are the ones to provide it. She has just forced the Bayport Museum to return her family's art collection to her—a collection that includes the infamous Borgia dagger. Legend says that if its owner touches the dagger, he (or she) will die within weeks.

Tessa has touched the dagger, and now she's become the target of many dangerous accidents. But there is more menace in Tessa's life. A disgruntled former servant has been threatening her; an old family friend nearly poisons her; even Tessa's boyfriend may not have her best interests at heart. Frank and Joe must discover the true secret of the antique treasure—before it's too late for them all, in *The Borgia Dagger,* Case #13 in The Hardy Boys Casefiles.

Forthcoming Titles in the
Hardy Boys Case Files™

Simon & Schuster publish a wide range of titles from pre-school books to books for adults.

For up-to-date catalogues, please contact:

International Book Distributors
Campus 400
Maylands Avenue
Hemel Hempstead
Herts
HP2 7EZ

Tel. 0442 882255

Simon & Schuster are delighted to announce that they are continuing the immensely popular Nancy Drew Files series in the UK, and will be publishing two titles per month.

THE NANCY DREW FILES
– FEATURING THE POPULAR TEEN DETECTIVE – ARE BACK!

Forthcoming Titles